STEA|||

AROUND MIDDLESBROUGH

STEAM

AROUND MIDDLESBROUGH

MIKE HITCHES

AMBERLEY

Dedicated to the memory of Bernard Unsworth,
fellow railway enthusiast and good friend.

First published 2014

Amberley Publishing
The Hill, Stroud
Gloucestershire, GL5 4EP

www.amberley-books.com

Copyright © Mike Hitches 2014

The right of Mike Hitches to be identified as the Author
of this work has been asserted in accordance with the
Copyrights, Designs and Patents Act 1988.

British Library Cataloguing in Publication Data.
A catalogue record for this book is available from the British Library.

ISBN 978 1 4456 1524 0 (print)
ISBN 978 1 4456 1547 9 (ebook)

Typeset in 10pt on 12pt Sabon.
Typesetting and Origination by Amberley Publishing.
Printed in the UK.

CONTENTS

INTRODUCTION

The birthplace and cradle of modern railways was the north-east of England and the Middlesbrough area. Collieries had been established in the North East since the Industrial Revolution, and wagon ways were constructed, using horse power to transfer coal from pitheads to the coast for onward shipment to the capital and elsewhere.

Steam was already in use for operating stationary pumps, which were used to remove water from the mines themselves, but it wasn't until Richard Trevithick had built a simple steam road vehicle at Coalbrookdale, Shropshire, in 1802 that interest in mobile steam power began to be seriously considered. He built his first steam locomotive for the Penydarren plateway, South Wales, in 1804, and it successfully hauled a heavy coal train, but broke the iron plate rails due to its weight. However, this experiment proved the viability of steam power, although it would take a few years before it replaced traditional horse power.

The impetus for investment in steam came during the Napoleonic Wars, which saw a massive increase in the cost of horse fodder. Within ten years, there had been major strides in the development of the steam locomotive. Interest in steam traction from the public was fostered by Richard Trevithick's 'Catch Me Who Can' demonstration, for which he had a steam loco running round in a circle at Euston Square, London, in 1808. By 1812, one John Blenkinsop had developed 'rack and pinion' steam locos, which operated on the Middleton Railway in Leeds. A similar system can be seen on the Snowdon Mountain Railway in North Wales. In the North East, William Hedley built *Puffing Billy* to work on the Wylam Colliery system, near Newcastle, in 1813.

Around the same time as Hedley was proving the value of the steam locomotive at Wylam, Northumberland, another son of the town, George Stephenson, was about to become the first great engineer of the railway age. Known as the 'Father of Railways', Stephenson was a self-taught engineer. Stephenson's father worked as a fireman for the Wylam Colliery stationary pumping engine, and George himself worked as a brakesman on the steam pumping engines while studying at night classes to read, write and learn mathematics. He was appointed engineer at Killingworth Colliery in 1813, and his first steam locomotive, *Blücher*, was built at the colliery workshop behind his home in 1814. In 1820, he built the Hetton Colliery Railway, a combination of rope-hauled inclines and steam-loco-hauled sections, the first railway which did not use horse power.

In 1821, Stephenson was appointed Chief Engineer of the newly promoted Stockton & Darlington Railway, and he opened his own locomotive works at Newcastle in 1823. He then went on to be involved in the building of the first truly intercity railway, the Liverpool & Manchester, in 1830. Indeed, his famous locomotive *Rocket* won the Rainhill Trials, near Liverpool, the previous year, running at 29.1 mph, a dazzling speed in those days.

The Stockton & Darlington Railway (S&DR), the first public railway in the world, was conceived by Edward Pease, a local wool merchant, and it received royal assent in 1821. On the same day, George Stephenson persuaded Pease to allow him to resurvey the proposed route and, at least partly, for it to be worked by steam. A new Act was obtained that approved these changes, and a clause was added that allowed use of locomotives or 'moveable engines'. The Act also made provision for transport of passengers, which, at that time, was to be a sideline only. The main purpose of the line was to transport coal from the collieries in the West Auckland area to Stockton-on-Tees for onward shipment by sea. John Lambton, later Earl of Durham, inserted a stipulation that limited charges for transit of coal to Stockton for onward shipment to ½d a ton per mile, compared to land shipment of 4d a mile, as a way of protecting his own exports from Sunderland. This arrangement would lead to the ultimate success of the S&DR.

The first locomotive to run on the S&DR was *Locomotion No. 1*, which was built at the Stephenson works and maintained at the S&DR works at Shildon, although the loco was put on tracks and tested at Newton Aycliffe, where, interestingly, the new Hitachi railway factory is to be built. It was *Locomotion No. 1* that hauled the first passenger train when the S&DR was officially opened on 27 September 1825. Most of the 600 passengers were carried in open coal wagons, while the dignitaries were carried in an experimental passenger coach, the whole 12-mile journey taking some two hours. Soon afterwards, a regular passenger service was established, using a horse-drawn coach. Such services were contracted out, but locomotive-hauled coal trains were paid for by the ton, and contractors provided their own fuel.

In 1831, Middlesbrough became part of the infant railway network when the S&DR extended its line from Stockton. At that time, Middlesbrough was no more than a small fishing community, but it did lie downstream from shallows that had to be negotiated by ships sailing from Stockton Wharf. Soon afterwards, ironstone deposits were discovered nearby and, along with coal, were brought to Middlesbrough by rail, allowing the establishment of a thriving iron and steel industry.

By 1833, the S&DR had become wholly run by steam traction and the company had become sole operator of the line, it having become double-tracked to allow trains to travel in opposite directions. Timetables were established, and crude signalling was introduced to prevent collisions. These were to become standard methods of railway operation throughout the world.

In the same year, the Clarence Railway (which had been incorporated in 1828) was opened to compete with the S&DR, and ran from Port Clarence, on the opposite bank of the River Tees, to the S&DR coal staithes at Port Darlington. The line then continued to a junction with the S&DR at Simpasture, south-east of Shildon, travelling via Haverton Hill, Billingham, Norton, Redmarshall (originally Carlton), and Stillington. Investors proposed that having a junction with the S&DR would allow the Clarence Railway to provide transport for Witton Park colliery. The Clarence Railway also had branches from Stillingmoor to Ferryhill, from Norton to Stockton, from Ferryhill to Coxhoe (opened 1834), and from Ferryhill to Byers Green (opened in 1837) and the Chilton branch. High charges from the S&DR, however, meant that the Clarence Railway never made any money.

The Clarence Railway itself was purchased by the Stockton & Hartlepool Railway (S&HR) on 30 June 1852, at the same time as it merged with the Hartlepool & West Harbour & Dock Company. The S&HR was the brainchild of Christopher Tennant, who came from Yarm and had previously opened the Clarence Railway in 1833. His idea was to extend the existing port at Hartlepool and develop new docks to serve the coal trade; the Hartlepool Dock & Railway Company was formed, and would fund a new railway, the S&HR, absorbing the Clarence Railway to extend it north, which would serve the new dock, creating a link to the Durham coalfield. Following the death of Tennant in 1839, running of the HD&R Co. was taken over by Stockton solicitor Ralph Ward Jackson, who oversaw construction of the S&HR from Hartlepool to Billingham, via Seaton Carew. He also agreed the junction of the S&HR with the Clarence Railway from 1840, which allowed passenger services to operate from Hartlepool to the S&DR at Stockton. By 1844, Jackson had agreed a twenty-one-year lease of the Clarence Railway to the HD&R Co. Frustrated at planning restrictions on the old Hartlepool docks and surrounding land for access, Jackson bought land, mostly sand dunes, to the south-west, and established West Hartlepool. So successful was the shipping of coal from West Hartlepool, via his West Hartlepool Dock & Railway Co. and the increasing size of shipping accommodated at the port, that the new town would eventually dwarf the old town. The 8-acre West Hartlepool Harbour & Dock Co. itself was opened on 1 June 1847.

An early branch from Middlesbrough was the Middlesbrough & Redcar Railway (M&RR), which was authorised by an Act of 21 July 1845 and opened to passengers less than a year later, on 5 June 1846. Along with passenger services, the line was an important goods route. To serve extra traffic generated by the new branch, the original Middlesbrough station was replaced by a new one in 1847. Some thirty years later, in December 1877, the present station was opened.

The M&RR was leased to the S&DR on 1 October 1847, and the two were amalgamated on 30 June 1862. The whole of the S&DR was absorbed by the North Eastern Railway on 13 July 1863, along with the Clarence and Hartlepool railways. Before NER control, the M&RR was extended to Saltburn in 1861.

An extension south to Loftus, via Brotton and Carlin How, was built by the Cleveland Railway in the 1860s, where it was to make a head-on connection with the Whitby, Redcar & Middlesbrough Union Railway, creating a railway connection to Whitby. However, due to construction and financial problems, the line from Whitby was not completed until December 1883. Some two years later, on 16 July 1885, the line from Whitby to Scarborough was completed, giving Middlesbrough full access to the North Yorkshire Coast seaside resorts, both railways having been completed under the auspices of the NER.

Another line from Middlesbrough was the Middlesbrough & Guisborough Railway (M&GR), which had been supported by Joseph Pease, who had iron-ore interests in the locality, and promoted by the S&DR, who worked the line and absorbed it in 1858. The M&GR opened to an iron-ore mine at Codhill in 1853, passenger services commencing a year later. Stations were situated at Ormesby, Nunthorpe, and Pinchingthorpe, the line terminating at Guisborough. The Cleveland Railway also served Guisborough, via a branch a little further along the S&DR, although this line was abandoned south of Ormesby after absorption by the NER. The NER then connected the line east of Guisborough to the M&GR, which meant that trains had to reverse out of the terminus station before continuing on to Loftus. Guisborough and the M&GR were connected to the Loftus line from 1861. A branch between Nunthorpe and Battersby, where it connected with what was to become the Esk Valley line, was built in 1865.

The Esk Valley line itself has a long history. The first section between Whitby and Grosmont dates back to the early years of Britain's railways, having been opened in 1835. The second section ran east from Picton, on the Northallerton–Eaglescliffe line, and was built by the North Yorkshire and Cleveland Railways and was opened to mineral traffic as far as Battersby on 6 April 1858, and to passengers from Stokesley to Castleton on 1 April 1861 after the line had become part of the NER empire from 1858. The section between Grosmont and Castleton was completed as late as 2 October 1865.

With completion of these lines, the railway system around Middlesbrough was virtually complete and now under the full control of the NER, which was to become a wealthy company due to its connections with coal and ironstone mines, shipbuilding further north in places like Sunderland and Newcastle-upon-Tyne, and the seaside resorts at places like Saltburn, Whitby and Scarborough. With so much coal and mineral traffic in the Middlesbrough locality, many of the loco sheds established here contained freight engines, along with tank locos for local passenger traffic and shunting duties in the many goods yards. Longer-distance passenger engines were usually stabled in sheds at Darlington, Stockton and Middlesbrough for express services emanating from these towns.

At the beginning of the twentieth century, the NER remained busy with freight and passenger traffic in the Middlesbrough area, but clouds were gathering, and when war finally broke out, in August 1914, all railway companies were brought under the control of the Railway Executive for the duration of hostilities. From this point until the Armistice in 1918, the railways came under severe pressure. Indeed, Hartlepool itself, along with Whitby and Scarborough, was shelled by the German navy in December 1914, while the Royal Navy remained complacently in port; this resulted in many casualtiesAs the NER served the many collieries and shipyards in the north-east of England, its tracks became used beyond capacity, and maintenance of the infrastructure suffered due to lack of manpower; many of the workers had volunteered for the army. Like other industries, men were replaced by women, who filled gaps in the railway workforce as ticket collectors, porters, and cleaners in loco sheds and many other essential railway works.

After cessation of hostilities, a short-lived economic 'boom' followed as the nation recovered and attempted to bring its infrastructure back to pre-war conditions. At the same time, however, this was a period of industrial unrest, culminating in a national railway strike in 1919. During the same period, the railway companies were inadequately compensated for their war efforts and there was also agitation for them to be nationalised. The post-war government did not favour state control of the network in peacetime, but did investigate the possibility of the wholesale 'Grouping' of 120 various railway companies, which culminated in the Railways Act of 1921. The Act envisaged that these companies would be reorganised into four groups, and the changes would take effect from 1 January 1923.

Thus, the NER, along with the Great Northern, Great Central, Great Eastern, Hull and Barnsley, North British and Great North of Scotland, would become a constituent of the new London & North Eastern Railway (LNER). At the same time, the economic 'boom' was now coming to an end, and industrial unrest continued to affect the nation, culminating in the 1926 General Strike. Workers, including railwaymen, went on strike for eight days in support of the coal miners, who had suffered severe pay reductions in the post-war years. While the General Strike was over after eight days, the miners stayed out for several months more, meaning lost revenue for the LNER, among others in mining districts. Further problems were to follow for the LNER in the north-east and Middlesbrough areas following the 1929 Wall Street Crash in New York, which led to the Great Depression of the 'Hungry Thirties'. Collieries and shipyards closed as Britain became uncompetitive in the world, and internal demand fell, which meant the LNER lost substantial freight revenue. Along with the loss of freight income, passenger demand fell as unemployment continued to rise throughout the decade and incomes were reduced. The situation only improved as the decade drew to a close and ended with the outbreak of the Second World War on 3 September 1939.

Once again, the railways came under pressure as they reverted back to state control. Furthermore, the system was a target for German bombers. As the Middlesbrough area was a centre of coal, steel and chemical industries, air raids were not uncommon. Indeed, Middlesbrough station itself received a direct hit in a daylight raid in August 1942, killing eight people. A plaque was unveiled at the station seventy years later to commemorate the victims of this attack.

The war in Europe came to an end in May 1945, and a Labour government was elected by a landslide a few months later. This new government favoured wholesale nationalisation of key industries, which included collieries and the railways, setting in place legislation to bring it about. The 1947 Transport Act envisaged nationalisation of the railways, road haulage, and buses to form an integrated transport system (something which is yet to be achieved) and the railways came under state ownership from 1 January 1948. The LNER was split into the Eastern and North-Eastern regions, while the Scottish components of the LNER, along with the LMS Scottish system, became the new Scottish region, with headquarters at York. The North-Eastern and Eastern regions were merged in 1967, with headquarters remaining at York. The new British Railways remained committed to steam traction because coal was plentiful and cheap, and the oil needed for diesel traction was expensive during these early post-war years. Rebuilding of the nation and bringing the railways up to pre-war standards was severely hindered when the USA called in its war loans, which left the UK with insufficient income to invest, and a period of austerity continued into the mid-1950s, with many goods remaining rationed during this period.

The post-war economic 'boom', with the export drive to earn hard currency, meant that unemployment was lower than it had been since the 1920s, which would have consequences for British Railways. Good steam coal was sent for export, leaving the railways with lower-quality material, which produced much dirty engine smoke and poor steaming, resulting in a dirty and unreliable railway. At the same time, new, clean industries were being created which attracted labour away from the railways and into this new world where wages were often higher, creating labour shortages in the dirty railway industry. As standards of living increased in the 1950s and 1960s, there was increasing car ownership, and new, cheaper road coaches could take passengers from door to door, rather than having to make onward connections from railway stations to final destinations. Also, there was an expansion of road haulage as surplus military vehicles were bought by ex-Army personnel who had learned to drive while on active service. These vehicles took freight away from the railways and, again, could provide a door-to-door service. Thus, railway income declined rapidly, and the infrastructure became shabbier as investment could not keep up with demand.

In an effort to turn around the fortunes of British Railways, two reports were to have an important effect on the system. The first was the 1955 Modernisation Plan, which envisaged replacement of steam with modern diesel and electric traction. Diesel multiple units began to appear soon afterwards, with diesel-electric locomotives hauling express services. Steam persisted on freight trains and substituted for failed diesel for a few years, but they had all gone from the main lines by 1968. Some found their way into preservation, and the North Yorkshire Moors Railway operates steam trains from Pickering to Grosmont, where it meets the Esk Valley line, sometimes operating steam trains to Whitby over the Esk Valley route.

The next report that would have a dramatic effect on the railway system was *The Reshaping of British Railways* by Dr Richard Beeching in 1963, which suggested wholesale closure of many loss-making branch lines and slimming down of some trunk routes, along with closure of around 2,000 stations. The Conservative Minister of Transport, Ernest Marples, had commissioned the report and, it could be argued, he had a vested interest in seeing the decline of the railway system, as he had interests in the civil engineering firm of Marples-Ridgeway, who were involved in road construction, particularly of the new motorways.

Some lines in the Middlesbrough area were closed even before Beeching's report, including Brusselton Land and the freight lines, which closed before 1955; the line from Loftus to Whitby (West Cliff) closed in 1958, which cut the coastal connection from Middlesbrough to Whitby; and Scarborough – its line from Whitby closed in 1965. Thus, there is now no rail connection along the coast from Scarborough; any passengers have to go via York and Middlesbrough and use the Esk Valley line, which leaves Whitby isolated from the main network. As part of the Beeching Plan, the line to Guisborough was closed in 1964, leaving Nunthorpe station to serve the Esk Valley line only. The famous S&DR remains open for the most part, but some sections have succumbed to Beeching.

Much of the railway system around Middlesbrough remains intact, serving industries in the area, but local stations have ceased to exist, like the steam locomotives which were a major part of the history of the area for some 150 years.

THE STOCKTON & DARLINGTON RAILWAY

Collieries in the Darlington area were landlocked, and coal had to be carried by horse panniers, which trebled the price at the pithead compared with that at Darlington. To reduce these prices, a canal was suggested as early as October 1768 by Robert Whitworth, who proposed one from Winston, 9 miles west of Darlington (which would not have served the coalfield at West Auckland directly), to Stockton. Nothing more was heard until 1810 when a suggestion for a railway from Winston to Darlington and Stockton was made by Leonard Raisbeck. However, a canal was offered as an alternative, and the famous engineer Rennie made a survey in 1813. He favoured a canal on the same course that had been recommended in 1768.

Nothing further was done until May 1818, when another survey was completed by George Leather. His plan, which did not find favour, would have bypassed Darlington and Yarm, and another survey was undertaken by Welsh engineer George Overton. His proposal was for a canal or railway, the latter estimated to cost £124,000, which would serve Darlington and pass close to Yarm. The population of Stockton favoured the scheme, which avoided Darlington, and battles between the two factions ensued.

Efforts by the Darlington faction ensured that Overton's proposal won the day, and his report was presented on 29 September 1818, with plans being deposited with Parliament by the end of October, even though a canal or railway had not yet been decided upon. The decision to construct a railway was taken on 13 November 1818, and £50,000 had been subscribed within a week. The Stockton faction itself favoured a railway, but it would have bypassed Darlington and gone no further.

The first S&DR Bill was narrowly rejected, and another application was made in 1820, but the death of King George II meant that this Bill had to be withdrawn. An Act was finally passed on 19 April 1821 which authorised a line from Witton

Park colliery to Stockton, along with five branches: to Yarm Bridge, Northgate Bridge (Darlington), Coundon turnpike, Evenwood, and Stockton.

Edward Pease was dissatisfied with Overton's survey, and, despite objections concerning extra costs, George Stephenson was engaged to do another. He submitted a modified route, requiring a new Act, which received royal assent on 23 May 1823 and included powers for the Croft branch (part of which remains as a section of the East Coast Main Line) and the Haggerleases branch. The S&DR itself was finally opened on 27 September 1825. On opening day, the first wagons were transported over the Etherley and Brusselton inclines using winding engines, and were attached to *Locomotion No. 1* at Masons' Arms level crossing at Shildon. A man on horseback carrying a red flag preceded the first train, which left, among cheers, for Stockton, arriving in the middle of the afternoon. As was usual on these occasions, a celebratory banquet followed at the town hall in Stockton.

When the S&DR began shipping coal from Stockton, there were problems with the shallow channel on the River Tees, and the company began to look for a more suitable wharf further along the river. Haverton Hill, on the north bank, was initially considered, but the eventual choice was the tiny village that was to become the great industrial town of Middlesbrough. The extension to Middlesbrough, on the south bank, was authorised on 23 May 1828 and opened on 27 May 1830, leaving the main line to Stockton at Bowesfield Junction and crossing the River Tees into Yorkshire on a suspension bridge. The bridge, however, was not a great success, because loads across it were severely restricted. This suspension bridge was replaced by a bridge with masonry piers and cast-iron girders in 1841. The new bridge had three river spans of 89 feet and two shore spans of 31 feet, with four girders for each span, the two lines being carried independently. When the bridge was replaced in 1907, the original piers and foundations were retained, and they continue in use today.

Opposite: A map of the S&DR with its extensions to Middlesbrough and Butterknowle as well as connections from the Leeds Northern Railway and the Clarence Railway at Stockton, while just to the right of the through station is the original S&DR terminus in the town. The map also shows George Hudson's Great North of England Railway between Darlington (Bank Top) and Aycliffe, which cut across the S&DR at right angles because he could come to no arrangement with the Darlington company. The flat crossing here survived well into East Coast Main Line days. For about eighteen months, the S&DR offered through tickets to the Tyne, but unsuspecting passengers found themselves forcibly ejected after around 12 miles at South Church, Bishop Auckland, and forced to take a horse bus to the next rail connection at Rainton Meadows. (Author)

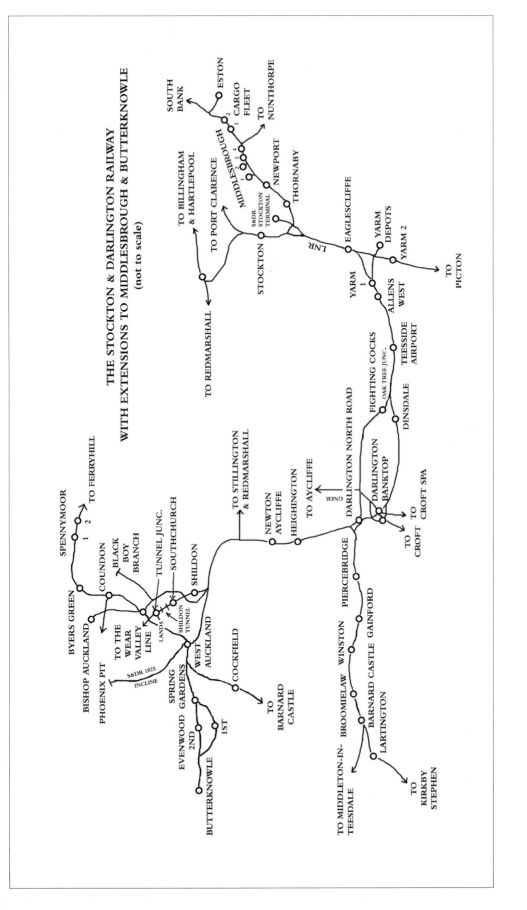

THE STOCKTON & DARLINGTON RAILWAY
WITH EXTENSIONS TO MIDDLESBROUGH & BUTTERKNOWLE
(not to scale)

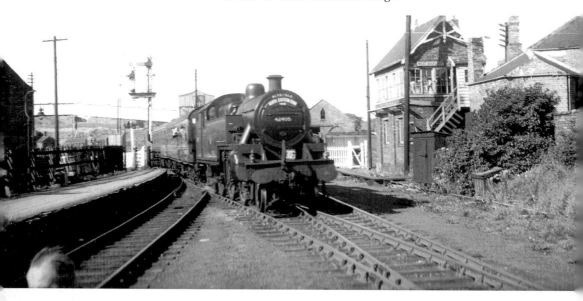

West Auckland station as it appeared on 30 September 1963, with an excursion train, headed by ex-LMS Fowler 2-6-4T No. 42409, approaching from Barnard Castle. When opened in 1825, the original main line connected Witton Park colliery with Stockton, and ran close to the village of West Auckland. On 1 October 1830, a branch line was opened from West Auckland to Hagger Leases Lane and started at a point known either as St Helen's Auckland or West Auckland, one village being on either side of the line. Originally, passenger services were operated by anyone who could run them, but the S&DR later decided to buy out these companies and run such trains themselves, beginning on 1 October 1833 between Stockton and Darlington, before being extended to Shildon and West Auckland on 1 December. The West Auckland station here was originally known as 'St Helens'. (R. Casserley)

	BISHOP AUCKLAND and BARNARD CASTLE.—North Eastern.												
Miles.	**Up.**	**Week Days.**						Miles	**Down.**	**Week Days.**			
		mrn	mrn	aft	aft		aft	aft	aft				mrn	mrn	aft	aft	aft	aft
	Bishop Auckland....dep.	6 52	10 8	1222	4 8		5 20	7 7	8 28		Barnard Castle........dep.	7 10	8 40	1240	2 55	4 30	6 15
2¼	West Auckland.........	6 59	1015	1229	4 15		5 27	7 14	8 35	7¼	Cockfield...............	7 26	8 56	1256	3 11	4 47	6 31
5¼	Evenwood...............	7 6	1022	1236	4 22		5 33	7 21	8 42	9¾	Evenwood...............	7 31	9 1	1 1	3 16	4 52	6 36
7¾	Cockfield...............	7 14	1030	1244	4 30		5 41	7 29	8 50	12¼	West Auckland.....[to 704	7 37	9 7	1 7	3 22	4 58	6 41
15	Barnard Castle *(above)*/arr	7 30	1045	1 0	4 45		5 55	7 44	9 5	15	Bishop Auckland 701 arr.	7 44	9 13	1 14	3 29	5 5	6 47

A 1910 NER timetable for passenger services between Bishop Auckland and Barnard Castle, via West Auckland. (Author's collection)

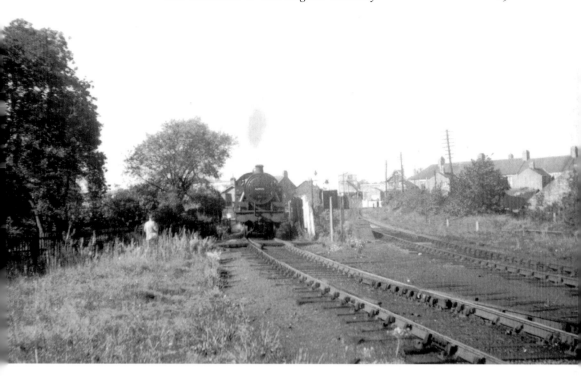

Another view of the excursion train of 30 September 1963, after the station had closed to passengers on 18 June 1962. The original route between Shildon and St Helen's Auckland ran over the Brussleton incline, where a winding engine had been installed to haul wagons up the steep inclines on each side. In the early days of the S&DR, a 1½-mile section of line that linked the Brussleton and Etherley inclines was worked by horses, and to carry the line over the River Gaunless here the first cast-iron bridge was built. When the bridge was replaced in 1901, the NER preserved the historic structure and it was a prized relic at the York museum, which had been established by the LNER in 1926 and is now called the National Railway Museum. In January 1842, the first section of the Bishop Auckland & Weardale Railway, from a junction with the S&DR near Shildon, including the 1,225-yard Shildon Tunnel, opened as far as South Church (and was later extended to Crook in 1843). A connecting spur from the north end of Shildon Tunnel allowed trains from St Helen's Auckland to reach Shildon without using the Brussleton incline; it was authorised on 4 July 1854 and opened on 13 September 1856. A line, proposed by the South Durham & Lancashire Union Railway, which began at a junction with the Haggerleases branch (opened to serve collieries at the head of the valley) and terminated at Butterknowle, at Spring Gardens Junction, was authorised in 1857. The section between St Helen's Auckland and Barnard Castle was opened on 1 August 1863, and a direct line between St Helen's Auckland and Bishop Auckland was authorised in 1858. St Helen's Auckland station was renamed 'West Auckland' on 1 March 1878. (R. Casserley)

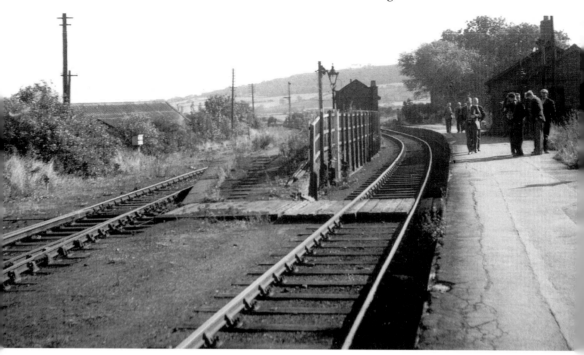

West Auckland station, looking in the direction of Bishop Auckland. Along with the station here, West Auckland was provided with a loco shed, situated on the north side of the line and east side of the station, between St Helen's colliery and the Dilks Street underbridge. It was of the roundhouse pattern with a single turntable. At the end of 1920 there were twenty-two locos allocated to West Auckland, fifteen of which were NER Class P1 0-6-0s, West Auckland being a sub-shed of Shildon. At the Grouping, there were twenty-nine locos allocated to West Auckland, which was now responsible for sub-sheds at Wearhead, Wear Valley Junction and Stanhope. West Auckland shed was closed in April 1931, and some of its engines transferred to Shildon. However, when sheds at Wear Valley Junction and Shildon were closed in July 1935, West Auckland was reopened. At nationalisation, thirty-seven engines were allocated to West Auckland, mainly five Class A8 4-6-2Ts, as well as twelve Class J25 0-6-0s; one Class J21, No. 5064, was allocated to the sub-shed at Wearhead. In 1949, BR allotted the shed code 51F, the 51 denoting the Darlington district. By 1950, the shed had an allocation of forty locos, and by 1959 there were only thirty-five engines at West Auckland, including seven J39 0-6-0s, six J72s, six Q6 0-8-0s, and six BR 'Standard' Class 4 2-6-0s. The shed remained open until February 1964, when the allocation was only twelve engines, which were transferred elsewhere.

In 1949, allocations at West Auckland was as follows:

J39 0-6-0	64778, 64848.
J21 0-6-0	65037, 65057, 65061, 65064, 65077, 65084, 65092, 65097, 65102.
J25 0-6-0	65659, 65662, 65671, 65675, 65683, 65696, 65706.
G5 0-4-4T	67294, 67312, 67345.
Y1 (Sentinel)0-4-0T	68142, 68145, 68149.
Y3 (Sentinel) 0-4-0T	68182.
J71 0-6-0T	68249, 68254, 68255, 68269.
J77 0-6-0T	68391.
J72 0-6-0T	68691, 68696, 69007.
A8 4-6-2T	69856, 69868, 69870, 69872, 69875, 69886.

Total: 39. (R. Casserley)

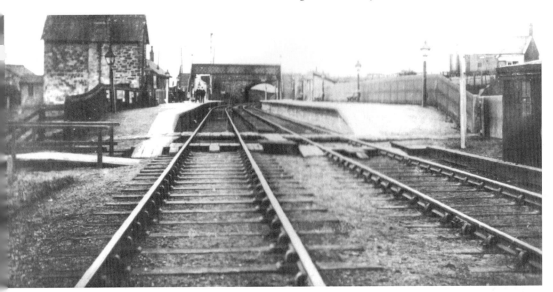

Running south-west from West Auckland was the branch to Barnard Castle. One of the stations on the branch was at Cockfield, seen here at the end of the nineteenth century. (LOSA)

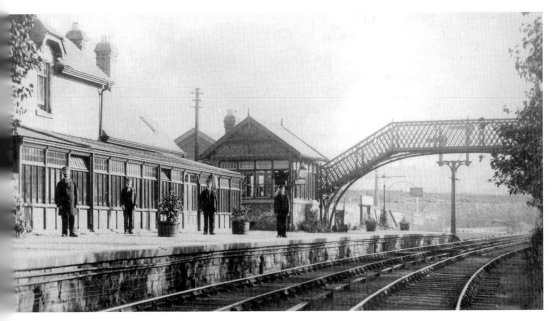

Coundon station, north of Shildon, with staff at the end of the nineteenth century. Although a branch to Coundon was authorised in the original S&DR Act of 1821, progress was blocked by a range of hills over 500 feet high north of Shildon, and nothing was done until it was certain that the S&DR was to be a success. Thus, the Black Boy Branch, which served local collieries, was not opened until 1827. The inclines on the Black Boy Branch became redundant when Shildon Tunnel was opened in 1842, but they were retained to serve the collieries on the branch. In the same year, the S&DR attempted to obtain a north–south passenger service to a temporary terminus at South Church. From 1 May 1842, a horse bus service connected with the terminus of the Durham Junction Railway at Rainton Meadows. (LOSA)

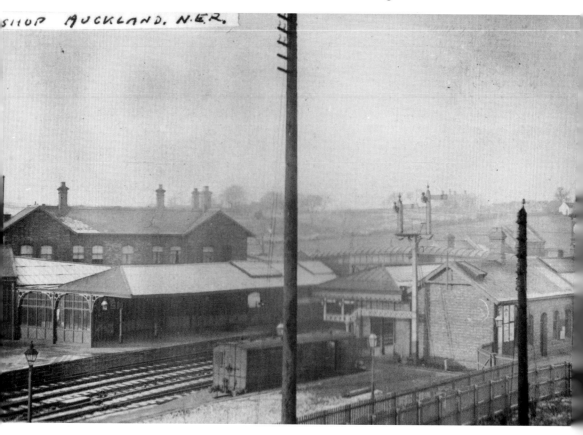

SHOP AUCKLAND. N.E.R.

Bishop Auckland station at the end of the nineteenth century, built by the Bishop Auckland & Weardale Railway, which was itself taken over by the Wear Valley Railway, the Weardale Extension Railway and the Wear & Derwent Railway under an Act of 22 July 1847. The Wear Valley Railway was then leased to the S&DR for 999 years from 1 October 1847. Thus, Bishop Auckland was a junction for lines to Coundon, Durham, Crook, the Wear Valley and Barnard Castle, via West Auckland. (LOSA)

Opposite top: North of Coundon stood the station at Byers Green, seen here at the end of the nineteenth century with the goods shed curving away to the left. An engine shed was opened in 1878 and was 1 mile west of Burnhouse Junction, where the West Durham Railway and Clarence Railway made a head-on junction. Byers Green station was some distance away and was on a later line from Burnhouse Junction to Bishop Auckland, via Coundon. The three-road brick-built loco shed accommodated some eight mineral engines of NER Class 398 – Nos 163, 488, 941, 990, 1372, 1374, 1386 and 1455 – which were there between 1920 and 1922. Nos 1372, 1374 and 1455 were withdrawn in 1920, and No. 941 was scrapped in 1921. To the four remaining engines were added another Class 398 loco, No. 1405, and a P2, No. 406, these six being allocated there when the shed closed on 17 July 1922. After many years out of use, the building was eventually sold for use as a brickworks. (LOSA)

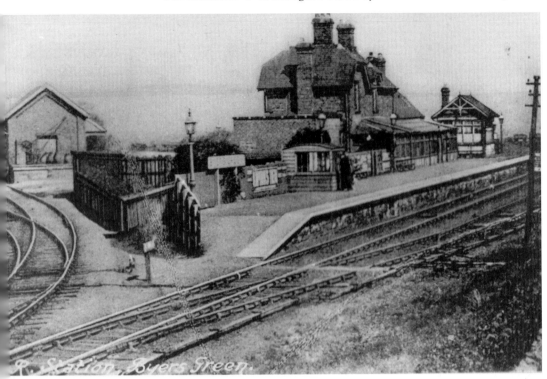

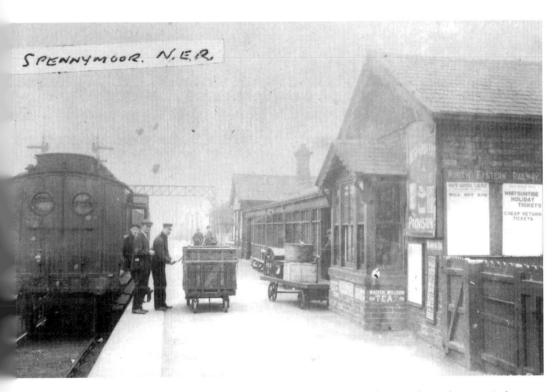

Curving round towards Ferryhill stood Spennymoor station, seen here early in the twentieth century as parcels are being loaded. (LOSA)

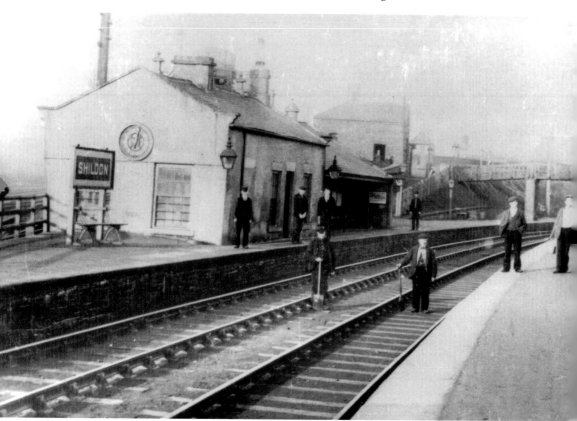

Shildon railway station and staff at the end of the nineteenth century. Shildon was the terminus of the S&DR when the railway was opened in 1825. A little over a year after the S&DR had opened, the improvement in transport brought about by the railway had reduced coal prices in Stockton by some 33 per cent, and within a further fifteen months they had more than halved. The new markets for coal in North Yorkshire and Darlington that were opened up by the railway created a dramatic increase in mining activity in the Auckland area, which also increased the prosperity of the S&DR. Edward Pease had forecast a 5 per cent interest on capital invested in the first year of operation, but within a decade this had increased to 14 per cent. Such was the success of the S&DR that the rest of the country, particularly industrialised areas, were keen to learn how to build and operate their own railway systems. (LOSA)

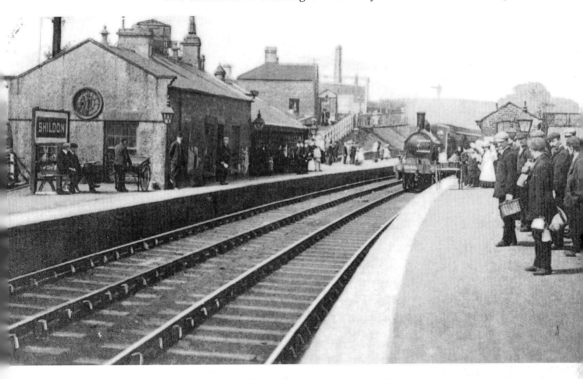

A North Eastern Railway train is approaching Shildon station early in the twentieth century as men from the railway works wait to go home after their shift has finished. The substantial marshalling yards are just visible in the left background, serving the works and loco shed, as well as a distribution centre for traffic from collieries in the West Auckland/Bishop Auckland area. As it was the terminus of the S&DR in its early years, the first locomotive superintendent, Timothy Hackworth, maintained the company's locos at the Soho works, Shildon. These steam engines had given so many problems that the company's directors were considering abandonment of steam traction. To try and solve these problems, Hackworth asked the company for a free hand to build a locomotive of his own design and, in 1827, he built the *Royal George*, which, among other innovations, introduced the blast pipe; this directed exhaust steam into the chimney, which drew the fire. So successful were these engines that seven more were built by 1832. When the S&DR no longer allowed horse-drawn passenger trains to be used, what steam locos there were, which tended to be freight engines, were slow, so Hackworth was asked to develop an engine that was faster and lighter than the freight locos currently in use. Thus, in 1830, the *Globe* was constructed as the first specialist passenger engine. The loco was reputedly the first to successfully use cranked axles. The S&DR purchased the Soho works in 1855 to become part of the Shildon and Darlington works. In 1863, the S&DR became part of the North Eastern Railway, and ten more locos were built there between 1863 and 1867, but most of this work was transferred to Darlington. By 1871, all locomotive construction ceased, and the original Soho works was closed in 1883. The remainder of the Shildon works continued as a major centre for wagon building and repairs. Its most famous freight vehicles built in the twentieth century were the 'Presflo' cement wagons and 'Freightliner' container wagons. As BR freight traffic declined, demand for wagons fell and the works closed in 1984. Part of the works remains in existence as the Shildon Locomotion Museum, which is operated by the National Railway Museum in conjunction with Durham County Council. (LOSA)

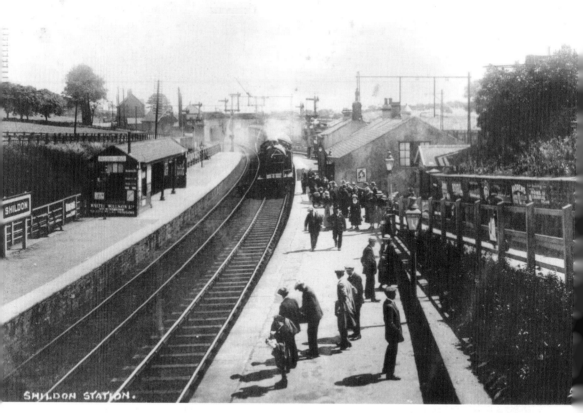

SHILDON STATION.

Another view of Shildon station looking in the opposite direction, with the locomotive works in the background and a train approaching as workers wait after work. As the works was established here, a loco shed was proposed on 1 January 1848, and was to hold six–eight engines 'with proper coke depots, furnace, and sand drying place, with water laid on'. This proposal was approved and, by 1849, a nine-road straight shed was situated immediately west of Mason's Arms level crossing. In 1852, a building for washing of locos was erected. By 1853, a new shed was authorised, at a cost of £2,345 7s 2d, and opened in April 1854, probably the first roundhouse. A further shed, to hold twenty-four engines, was authorised in June 1856 and a tender for another roundhouse was accepted in December 1864 at a cost of £3,916 5s 5d. In the 1870s, three circular sheds were in existence and, by 1866, a start was made on extensive rebuilding. A new turntable was ordered for No. 1 shed in 1886 at a cost of £388, and No. 2 and No. 3 sheds were rebuilt in 1891 and 1892, but the turntables were not renewed until 1906 when a 50-foot model was ordered for £870. In 1915, No. 3 shed was adapted to house ten electric locomotives to work the line to Newport. These locos ceased working in 1935, and on 8 July 1935 the shed was closed and its allocation of steam locos dispersed.

The allocation at closure was as follows (LNER numbers):

J21 0-6-0	16, 93, 582, 944, 1323, 1507, 1550, 1553.
J25 0-6-0	1973, 2054.
J27 0-6-0	1015, 1029, 1221.
J71 0-6-0T	40, 241, 802, 977.
Y3 0-4-0T	148.

Total: 18. (LOSA)

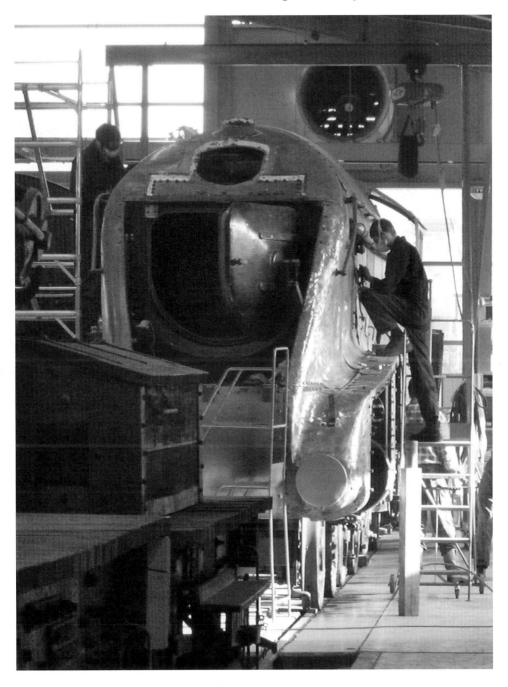

In July 2013, celebrations were underway to celebrate the seventy-fifth anniversary of LNER A4 Pacific *Mallard* and its speed-record-breaking run. The proposal was for every preserved A4 Pacific to be gathered together at the NRM's York museum for the celebrations, which meant that examples had to be brought back to the UK from the USA and Canada and restored to perfect external condition. The works at Shildon was to undertake the restoration of *Dominion of Canada*, and the following views show the work being carried out. Here, the smokebox is being cleaned and restored. She is still in the BR Brunswick Green livery used when operating on the East Coast Main Line. (Paul Hughes)

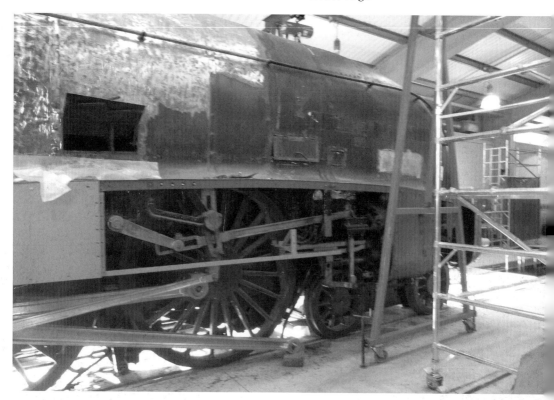

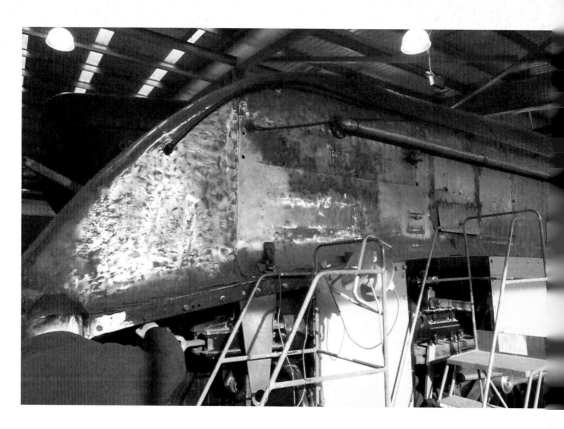

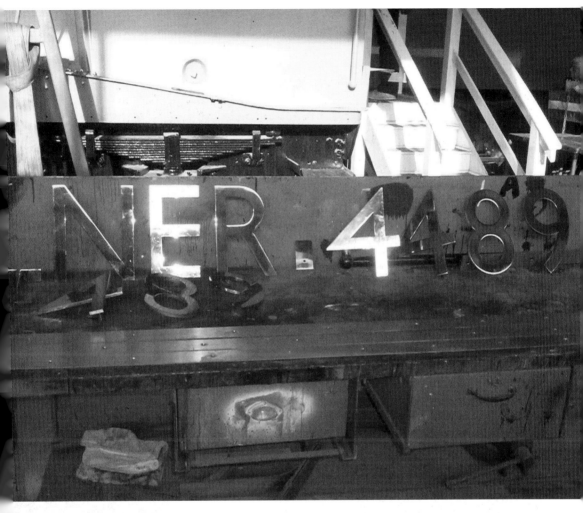

Stainless-steel LNER and 4489 name and number plates have been cut out and wait to be applied to *Dominion of Canada* as restoration continues. (Paul Hughes)

Opposite top: A side view of the front of the loco, with panels being restored. The wheels have been painted in LNER red and the running plate has the garter blue paint applied. (Paul Hughes)

Opposite bottom: New panels are being applied to the streamlined casing of *Dominion of Canada* at Shildon. (Paul Hughes)

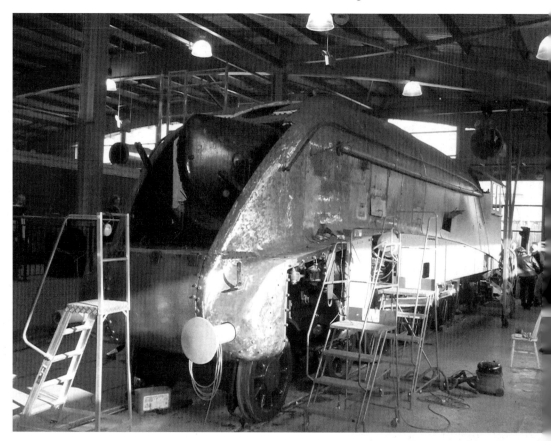

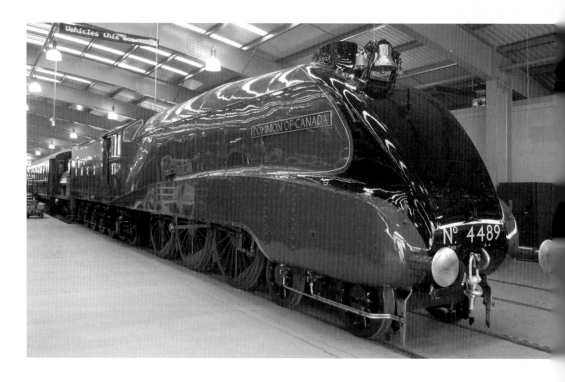

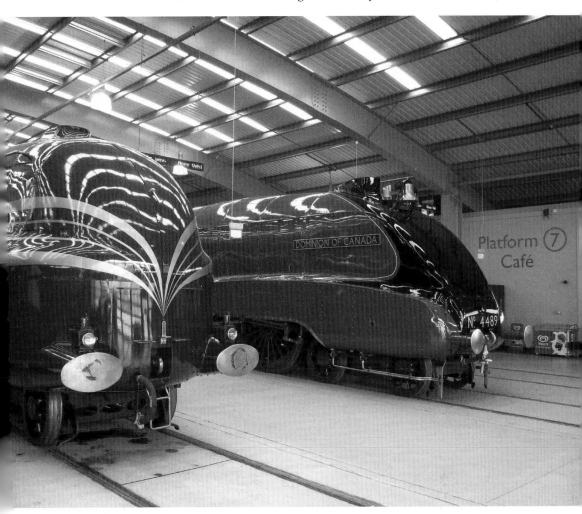

Looking resplendent at the Shildon museum, *Dominion of Canada* rests next to newly streamlined ex-LMS Duchess Pacific No. 6229 *Duchess of Hamilton*. The LMS loco was rebuilt into streamlined form at Tyseley works, Birmingham, and is a static exhibit at York. It was the competition between the LNER and LMS using these streamlined Pacifics that allowed speeds to increase (both classes having exceeded 100 mph in the late 1930s) until *Mallard* broke the steam speed record of over 126 mph in July 1938, hence the 'Mallard 75' celebrations. *Dominion of Canada* returned to the country after which she is named late in 2013 when the celebrations were over. It is to be hoped that the engine is being well looked after now that she has returned. (Paul Hughes)

Opposite top: A three-quarter view of the front nearside of *Dominion of Canada* as streamline panels continue to be replaced and finished. The smokebox door is in situ and is swung open. (Paul Hughes)

Opposite bottom: The finished A4 Pacific, No. 4489 *Dominion of Canada*, in LNER garter blue, with bell still attached to comply with Canadian railway regulations. A splendid job has been done, and the engine is a credit to all of those who restored it; she looked a picture next to the other A4s when on display at York. (Paul Hughes)

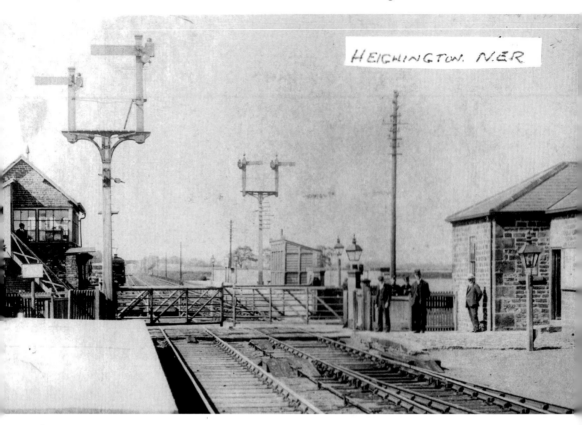

Between Shildon and Darlington, there were stations at Newton Aycliffe and Heighington; the latter is seen here at the end of the nineteenth century. Originally named Aycliffe Lane, the name was changed to Heighington to avoid a clash with Aycliffe station, which was situated on the Great North of England Railway line from York to Newcastle, later to become the East Coast Main Line. Heighington was the site of a locomotive boiler explosion on 1 July 1828, which caused one fatality. Boiler explosions were relatively common in the early days of the railways, as boilers were allowed to corrode and safety valves could be screwed down to increase locomotive performance, risking dangerous boiler pressures, which could cause such explosions. (LOSA)

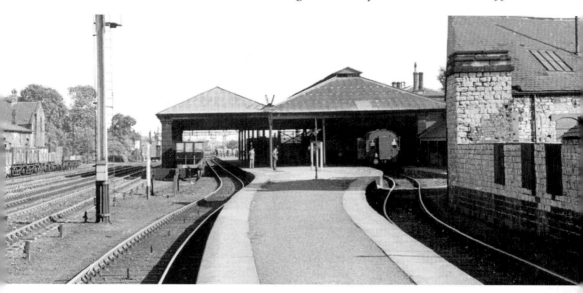

Darlington North Road station as it appeared on 30 September 1963, looking towards Bank Top station, on the East Coast Main Line. The North Road station seen here is the second, which was opened in 1842 to replace the original of around 1825. The original station stood east of the bridge over North Road, the old A1. The goods station was in a building with a clock tower above, and stood between the station and North Road. The original station was demolished in 1864 and the replacement North Road station is now a museum. (H. Casserley)

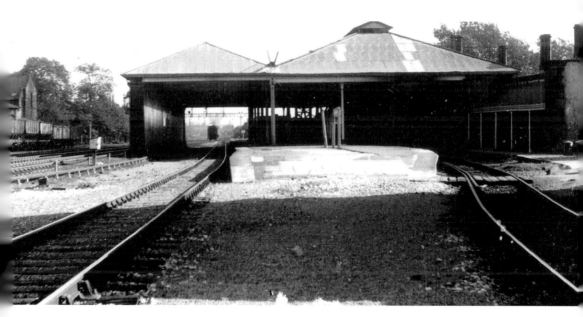

Another view of North Road station, with wagons in the sidings on the left. When the S&DR first opened, the railway crossed North Road on the level as it headed towards Stockton, but a bridge was provided in later years. At Darlington on 4 May 1851, there was a head-on collision between two trains, which caused fourteen injuries, but fortunately there were no deaths. Also, on 7 September 1863, a runaway train ran through Darlington, but it was stopped without any casualties. (R. Casserley)

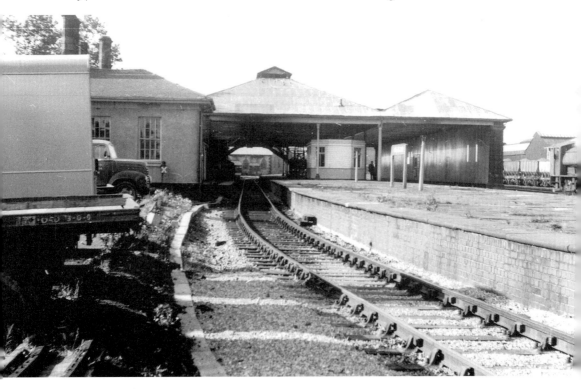

Darlington North Road station, looking in the direction of Barnard Castle, with an ex-LNER J94 0-6-0 saddle tank with a train of coal wagons heading towards Thornaby in September 1963. These saddle tanks were designed by Hunslets of Leeds for the military during the Second World War, and they could operate over tight curves on any railway system. Thus, they were ideal for use on the many colliery networks, and the LNER purchased several of them from the War Department after hostilities were over; they were a familiar sight on coal trains in the locality. (R. Casserley)

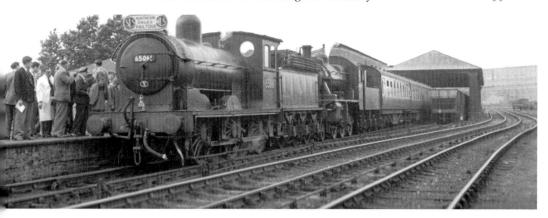

Standing at Darlington North Road station on 4 September 1955, after bringing in an excursion from Tebay, are ex-LNER Class J21 Worsdell 0-6-0 No. 65061 and ex-LMS Ivatt Class 2 2-6-0 No. 46478. (H. Casserley)

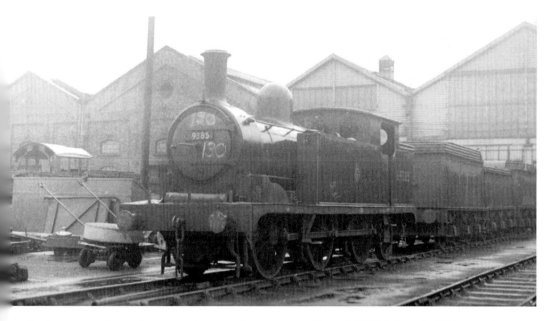

Darlington works as it appeared on 24 June 1950, with ex-LNER N8 0-6-2T No. 69385 awaiting repair. The works was opened in 1863 opposite to the line to Barnard Castle, and closed in 1966 after years of locomotive maintenance and construction. (H. Casserley)

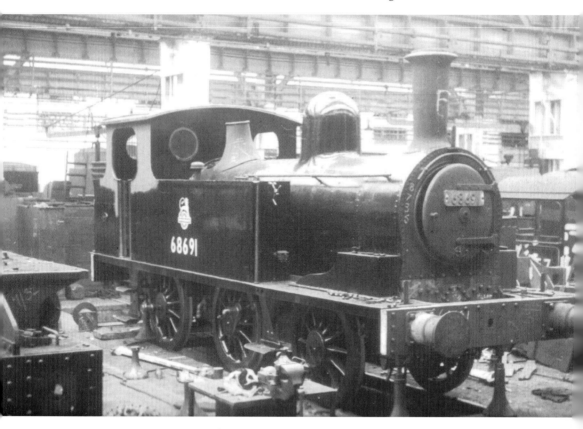

Interior of Darlington works in September 1955. Ex-LNER Class J72 0-6-0T No. 68691, after a heavy repair and repaint, is awaiting refitting of its coupling rods. (R. Casserley)

Opposite top: Outside the works are ex-WD J94 0-6-0ST No. 68008 and ex-LNER J71 0-6-0 No. 8239 on 24 June 1950. Although both engines are now owned by British Railways, the J71 retains its old LNER number. The S&DR also had a loco shed at Darlington North Road, which served lines running east to west (the NER Darlington shed provided engines for services running north to south). The shed was extended in 1859, and a new shed was authorised in 1860 and opened in 1861. North Road shed became more important when the new locomotive works was opened in 1863. On 17 August 1908, the shed building was badly damaged at the west end when Class U 0-6-2T No. 1138, hauling two Class P3 0-6-0 engines, collided with a Class E1 0-6-0T and knocked the latter broadside into the paint shop. A corner of the building had to be knocked down. The shed was demolished in 1933 to make way for improvements to the works yard. (H. Casserley)

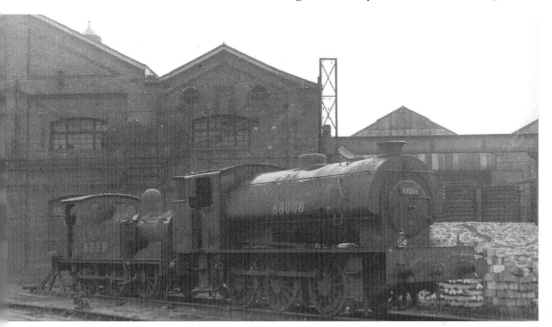

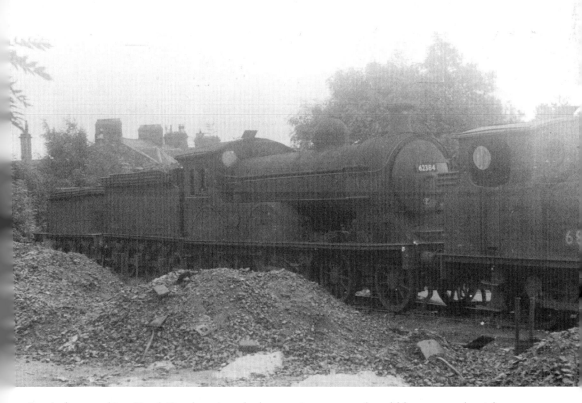

Just before reaching North Road station, the locomotive scrapyard could be seen on the right, and it was around here that the depots branch left the main line to reach the coal depots adjacent to Northgate Bridge. On opening day of the S&DR, six coal wagons were detached from the inaugural train and run on to the depots. The scrapyard is seen here on 4 September 1955, with ex-NER Class R (LNER Class D20) No. 62384 awaiting its fate. (R. Casserley)

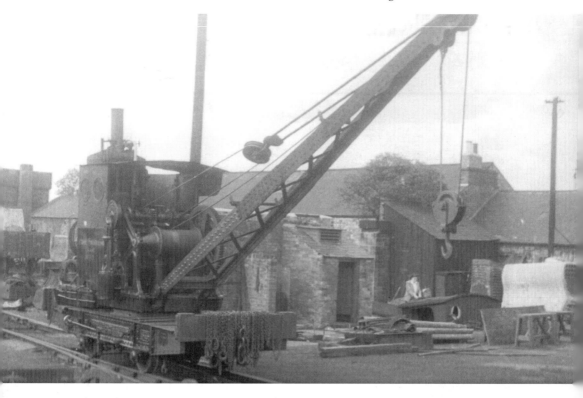

The rail steam crane at Darlington scrapyard in 1955. Old fireboxes can be seen in the background. (R. Casserley)

Opposite top: Just north of Darlington North Road station, the Barnard Castle branch headed west. The first station on the branch from Darlington was at Piercebridge, seen here early in the twentieth century. (LOSA)

Opposite bottom: From Piercebridge, the next station was at Gainford; its rural setting makes the station rather attractive. (LOSA)

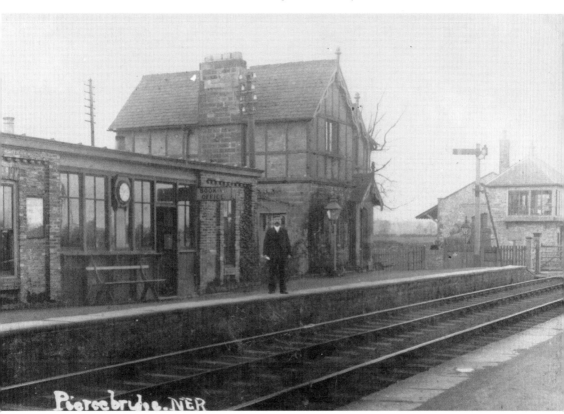

Piercebridge. NER

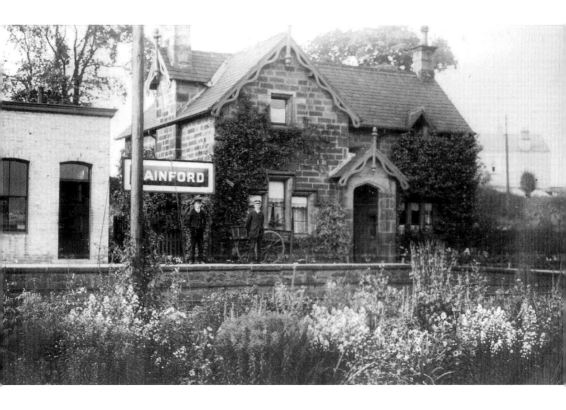

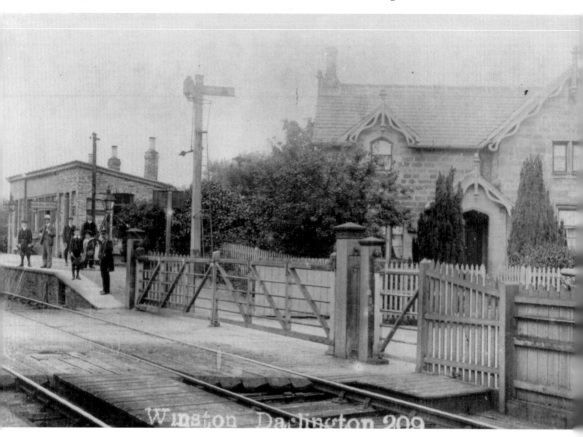

After leaving Gainford, the next station on the line was at Winston. Its simple platform building is on the left, and the attractive stationmaster's house, in typical NER style, is on the right. (LOSA)

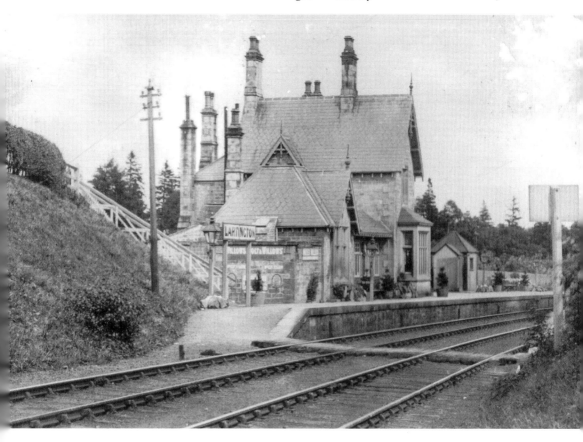

Between Winston and Barnard Castle, there was another station at Broomielaw. On arriving at Barnard Castle, there was a junction, one line going to Middleton-in-Teesdale and the other to Kirkby Stephen. The first station on the branch to Kirkby Stephen was at Lartington, and its substantial main building can be seen here in this early twentieth-century view. (LOSA)

DARLINGTON (Bank Top) and DARLINGTON (North Road).—North Eastern.

Down.	Week Days.																							Sundays.			
	mrn	mrn	m	mrn	mrn	mrn	mrn	mrn	mrn	aft	aft	aft	aft	aft	aft	m	aft	aft	aft					mrn	mrn	aft	aft
ng-{ Bank Top,......dep.	6 55	7 0	8 15	8 27	9 22	9c26	10 0	1032	1112	1240	1 20	2 3	7 4	10 5	3 5	8 6	127	27	7 32	1015	...	...	...	8 35	8 40	8 15	8 25
{ North Road ....arr.	6 59	7 4	8 19	8 31	9 26	9c30	10 4	1036	1116	1244	1 24	2 6	3 11	4 14	5 7	5 126	167	31	7 36	1019	...	...	...	8 39	8 44	8 19	8 29
Up.	mrn	mrn	mrn	mrn	mrn	mrn	mrn	mrn	mrn	aft	aft	aft	aft	aft	aft	m	aft	aft	m	aft	aft			mrn	mrn	aft	aft
ng-{ North Road.....dep.	7 20	8 15	8 27	8 52	9 48	9 52	10c30	1043	1149	1 6	1 48	4 9	4 15	4 40	5 41	6 25	6 46	7 55	9 17	9 26	1120	...	...	7 53	8 4	6 42	6·53
{ Bank Top.......arr.	7 24	8 19	8 31	8 56	9 52	9 56	10c34	1052	1153	1 10	1 52	4 13	4 19	4 44	5 45	6 29	6 50	7 59	9 21	9 30	1124	...	...	7 57	8 8	6 46	6 57

c Runs on the 13th and 27th instant.   m Auto-car.

A North Eastern Railway timetable for shuttle services between Darlington North Road station and Darlington Bank Top station. (Author's collection)

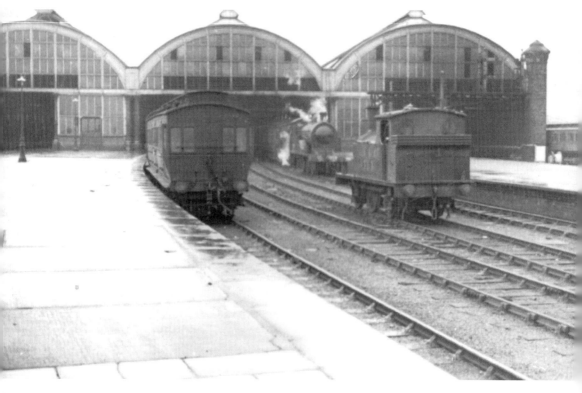

Darlington Bank Top station on 12 May 1938, with ex-NER Class R 4-4-0, as LNER Class D20 No. 1078 is waiting to depart with a southbound train, while LNER Class J71 0-6-0T No. 1797 is on station pilot duty. (H. Wheeller)

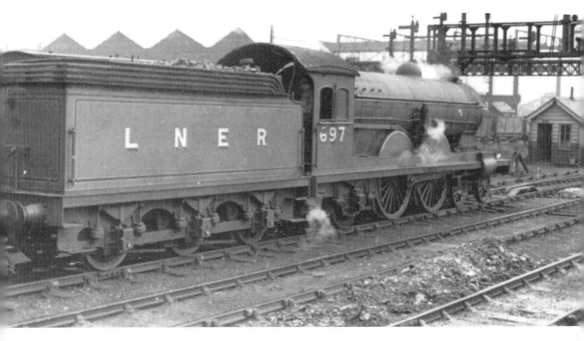

In the same year, LNER C6 4-4-2 No. 697 is waiting to depart from Darlington Bank Top station. (H. Wheeller)

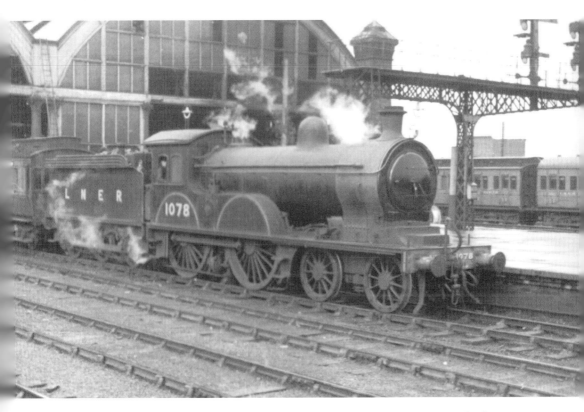

Another view of LNER D20 4-4-0 No. 1078 about to depart from the station. (H. Wheeller)

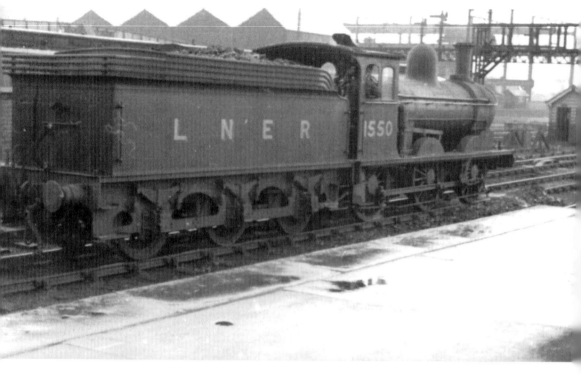

Ex-NER Worsdell Class J21 0-6-0, No. 1550, is awaiting its turn of duty at Darlington Bank Top station in 1938. (H. Wheeller)

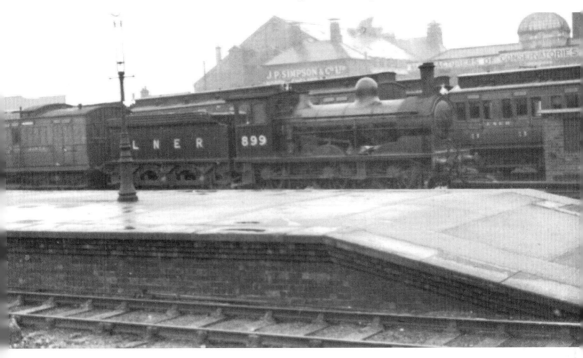

Another Class J21 0-6-0, No. 899, has recently arrived at Darlington Bank Top station in May 1938. (H. Wheeller)

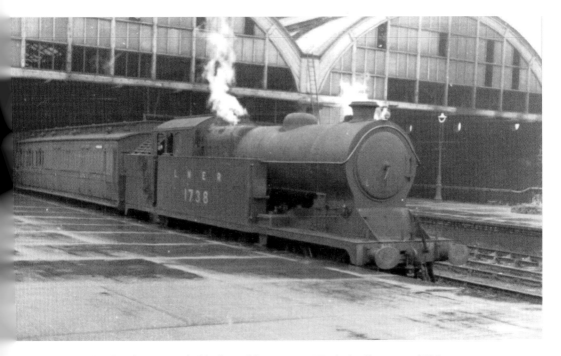

Waiting with a local train, probably for Saltburn, is LNER A5/2 Class 4-6-2T No. 1738 on 12 May 1938. This was one of a class of thirteen engines built by Gresley in 1925 for service in the Middlesbrough area. (H. Wheeller)

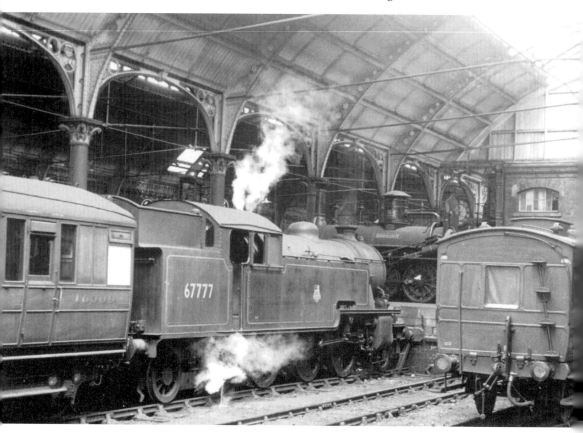

Darlington Bank Top station as it appeared in June 1950, with ex-LNER Class L1 2-6-4T No. 67777 at the buffer stops alongside ex-NER saloon No. 900272. Bank Top station was originally a modest structure and was rebuilt in 1860. A much more ornate station was opened by the NER on 1 July 1887. Just beyond the buffer stop, the famous S&DR *Locomotion No. 1* can be seen. The engine was initially preserved in 1857 and was set on a pedestal near North Road station until removal to Bank Top station in 1892. This famous loco is now preserved at the old North Road station museum. (H. Casserley)

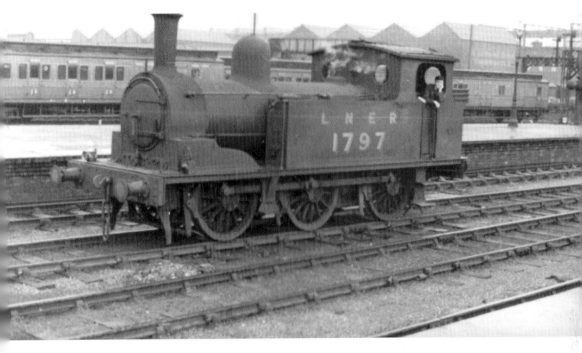

One of a class of 120 engines, ex-NER Worsdell 0-6-0T, as LNER Class J71 No. 1797, is seen on station pilot duty in 1938. (H. Wheeller)

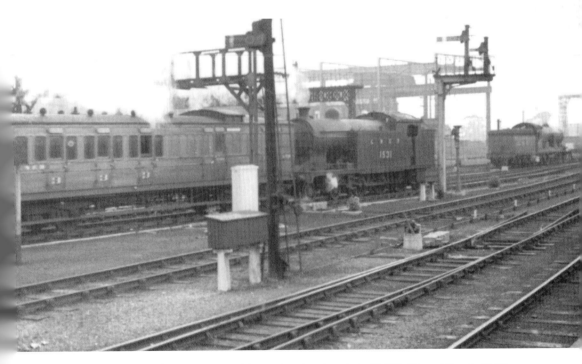

Leaving Darlington Bank Top station with another local train is LNER Class A8 4-6-2T No. 1531 on the same day. These A8 engines were rebuilds of ex-NER Class H1 4-4-4Ts, the conversions being carried out between 1931 and 1936. (H. Wheeller)

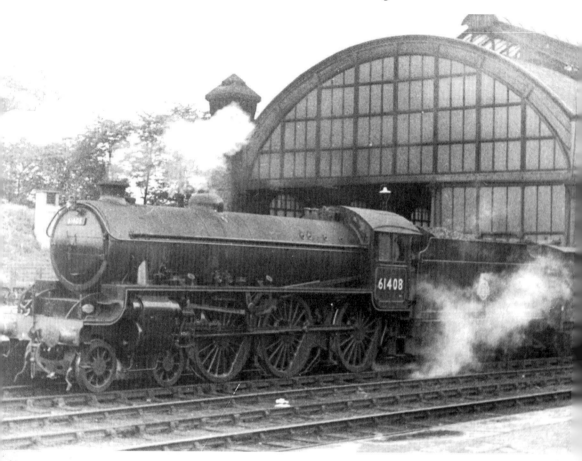

Bank Top station in June 1950, with ex-LNER B16 4-6-0 No. 61408 in charge of a fitted freight train. Over the years, several accidents have occurred around the Bank Top area. Early in the twentieth century, on 15 November 1910, the rear portion of an NER goods train from Parkgate to Hull, made up of twenty-eight wagons and a brake van, was standing on the Up main line at Darlington. It was run into by the 10.45 p.m. goods train from Newcastle to Leeds, which consisted of a loco, forty-eight wagons and a brake van. The speed of the latter train was between 30 and 40 mph. The engine of the Leeds train was thrown over on to its side to the west of the line on which it was running. The driver and fireman were killed instantly, and the brake van and five wagons of the Hull train were wrecked; eleven other wagons were severely damaged. The engine of the Leeds train was seriously damaged, two wagons totally wrecked and twenty seriously damaged. Five wagons on an adjacent line were slightly damaged. The cause was found to be driver fatigue or error. On 6 May 1872, there was a sidelong collision involving a passenger train and loose shunted van south of Bank Top station. An error by a guard was found to be the cause of the accident, as he intended to push the van along the south crossover towards an independent line but, in going to hold the points for the van to pass through to the south crossover road, he made the mistake of catching hold of the south points of the north crossover road instead of the north points to the south crossover. Therefore, the van passed southward along the Up main line and fouled the junction of that line with the Up line from Bank Top station. Along with guard error, the investigation also blamed a lack of interlocking there.

At 11.57 p.m. on 16 April 1904, the Down express from York to Newcastle, consisting of two engines and ten coaches, and running on the Down line between Darlington North and

South signal boxes, collided with a light engine that was standing on that line. The express was running at around 30 mph, and the driver of the light engine saw the train approaching and began to move his engine slowly forward at the point of impact. The rear portion of the light engine was lifted by the force of the collision on to the buffer beam of the express, but the leading wheels stayed on the rails, pushing the light engine some 320 yards as the express came to a stop. The rear end of the tender of the leading engine of the express was similarly lifted by the front end of the second loco and ran on locked together. The driver and fireman of the light engine both jumped clear just before the collision. The driver of the leading express engine suffered side bruising and the fireman chest, rib and facial injuries. Fortunately, there were no other injuries. The subsequent inquiry found that signalling errors, along with mistakes by the driver and fireman of the light engine, were the cause of the accident.

Perhaps the worst accident at Darlington was on 27 June 1928, which killed twenty-five passengers and seriously injured some forty-five more. A Class B16 4-6-0, No. 2369, was shunting a parcels train that it was due to work south when the driver overran a signal and stopped foul of the main line, over which a return excursion from Scarborough to Newcastle was due to pass; it was to run non-stop through Bank Top station and, headed by Class C7 4-4-2 No. 2164, was travelling at around 45 mph when it struck the engine of the parcels train, which was pushed back around 60 yards. Some of the passenger coaches were badly telescoped but, luckily, the wreckage did not catch fire, as had happened in previous collisions elsewhere, and this probably reduced the potential casualty levels. Along with these more serious events, there were smaller incidents, like a boiler explosion on 30 April 1877. (H. Casserley)

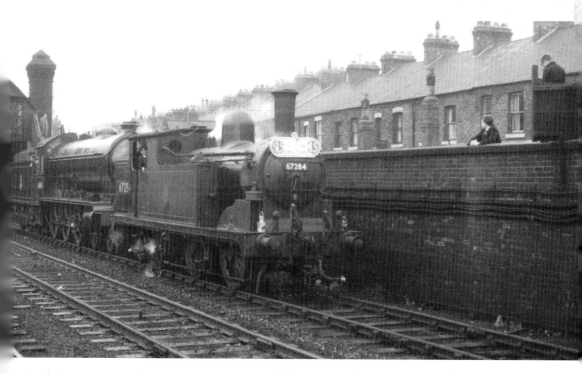

Bank Top station in September 1956, with ex-LNER G5 0-4-4T No. 67284 and B16 4-6-0 No. 61443 resting after bringing in an excursion train. When the new station opened, a new connecting line from the south end of the station at Polam Junction met the original S&DR line from Middlesbrough at Oak Tree Junction near Dinsdale, and the old line was closed to passengers, although it remained in use for freight until 1967. (H. Casserley)

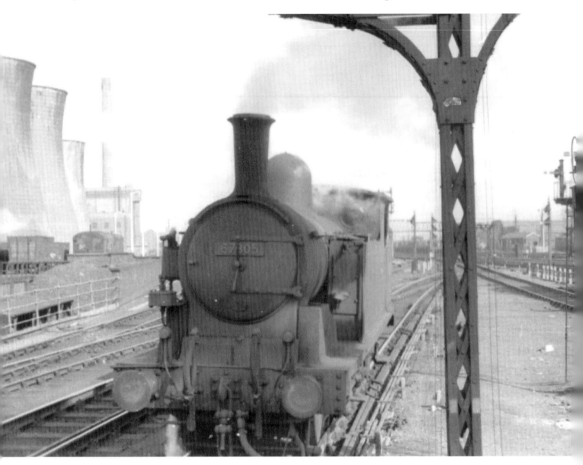

A view at the end of Darlington Bank Top station in September 1957 with ex-LNER G5 Class 0-4-4T No. 67305 departing for the loco shed after bringing in a local train. (R. Carpenter)

Opposite top: Ex-LNER Class J21 0-6-0 No. 65064 is standing outside Darlington Bank Top station in September 1957. (R. Carpenter)

Opposite bottom: Ready to depart with a local service in September 1957 is ex-LNER Class A5/2 4-6-2T No. 69830, one of the 1925-built batch. (R. Carpenter)

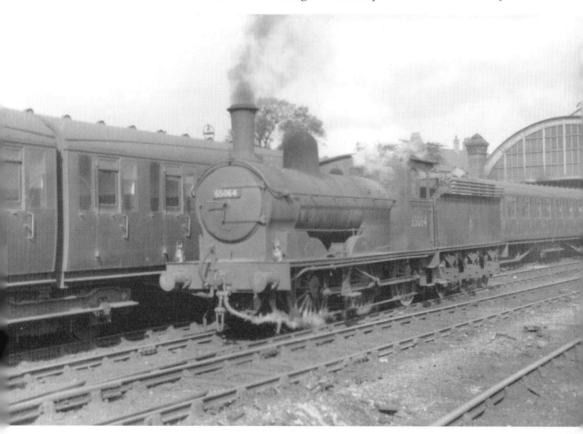

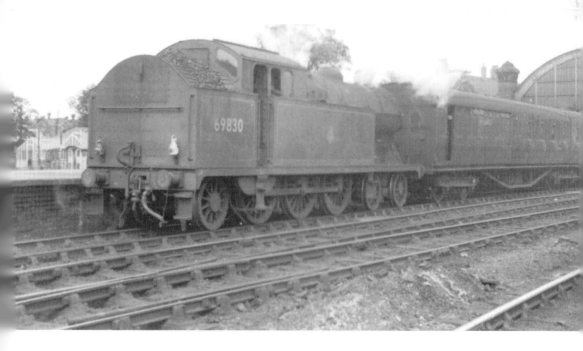

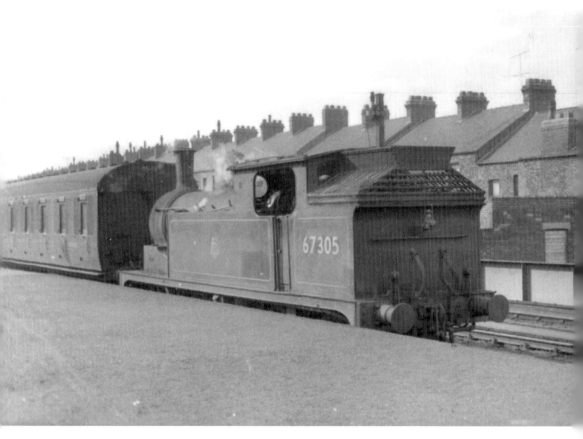

Waiting to depart Darlington Bank Top station with a local train, in 1957, is ex-LNER Class G5 0-4-4T No. 67035. (R. Carpenter)

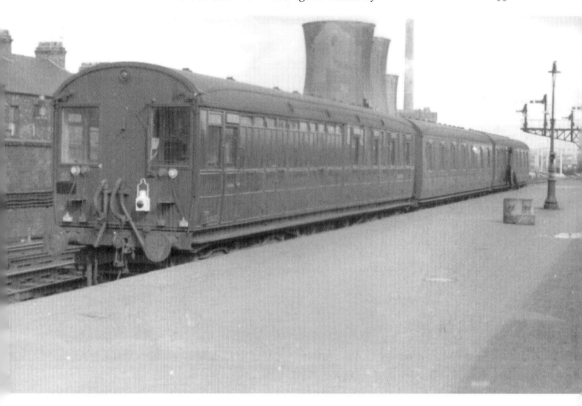

Waiting at Darlington Bank Top station in September 1957 is a rake of push-pull stock, which will make up a local service to Middleton-in-Teesdale. (R. Carpenter)

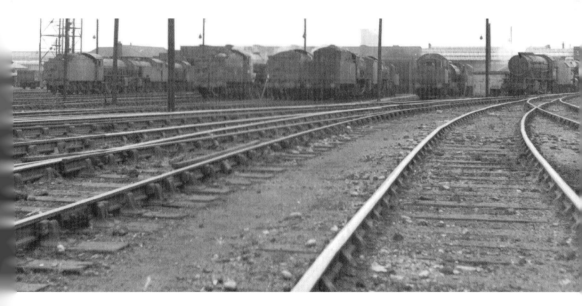

A general view of Darlington engine shed as it appeared on 2 July 1960, with several examples of ex-LNER and ex-WD tender engines in view. (R. Carpenter)

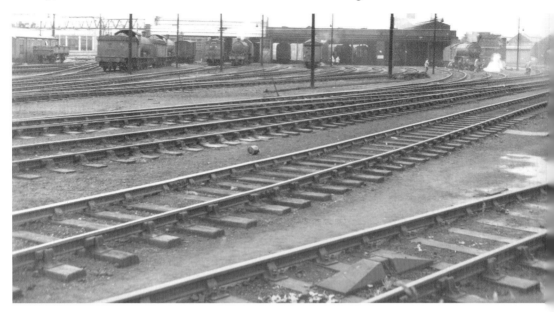

The same loco shed on 27 June 1964; several steam locos remain in view. (R. Carpenter)

Opposite bottom: The S&DR junction with the East Coast Main Line, just north of North Road station, seen here in September 1955 as an excursion train, running over the old S&DR route to Stockton-on-Tees, crosses the main line from Bank top to Durham (the original Newcastle & Darlington Junction Railway, which opened in 1844). The reason why this flat junction existed was due to the efforts of George Hudson, the famous 'Railway King', who promoted an extension to his Great North of England Railway, which ran from York to Darlington, to Newcastle. However, he could not come to an agreement with the S&DR, which lay at right angles to his proposed line, so he just drove through it. The resulting flat crossing of the two lines here survived on the ECML well into the twentieth century. As this junction now existed, for a year and a half the S&DR advertised its own through services from Darlington to Newcastle, but any intrepid passengers who attempted to use the service found themselves ejected from the train after less than 12 miles, at South Church, and forced to take the horse bus service to the next railhead at Rainton Meadows. The NER gave explicit instructions for working of this crossing, and instructed coal and mineral trains to give way to the passing of passenger trains. Every driver had to sound his whistle at least half a mile before reaching the crossing and continue to do so until the train drew the attention of the signalman. Speed over the crossing was limited to 10 mph; anyone disregarding these instructions had to be reported and the signalman was liable to a fine of five shillings if he failed to report any driver who did not follow the rules. (R. Casserley)

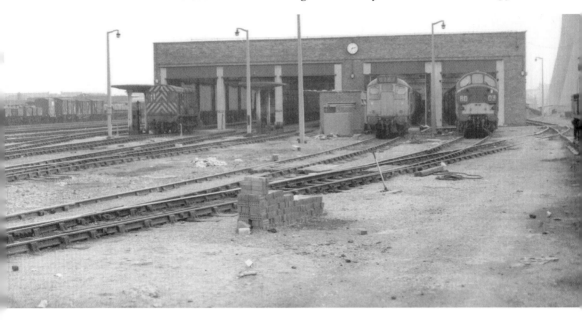

Some four years later, on 7 September 1968, the old steam loco shed has disappeared and been replaced by a BR-built diesel depot, seen here with a Class 08 diesel shunter on the left, a Class 31 in the centre and a Class 40 (or is it a Class 37?) on the right. (R. Carpenter)

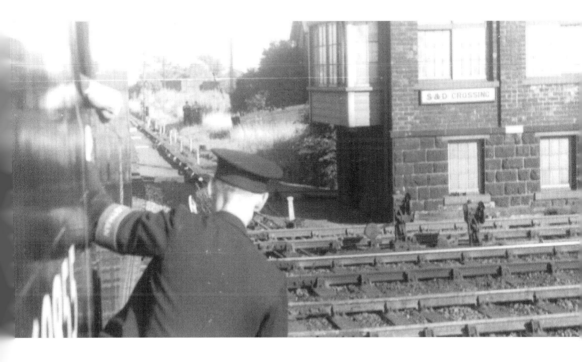

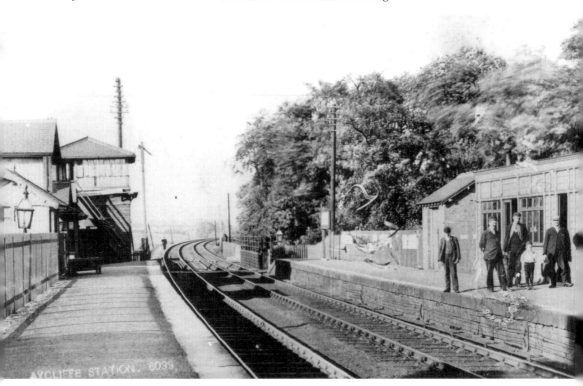

A little north of Bank Top station and the S&DR junction, on the ECML, was the station of Aycliffe, seen here at the beginning of the twentieth century, showing the buildings and signal box. It was the opening of this station that brought about the change of name of the S&DR station at Heighington. (LOSA)

Opposite bottom: Oak Tree Junction as it appeared on 4 September 1955. This was the point where the original S&DR line between North Road and Stockton met the new line from Bank Top, via Dinsdale. (R. Casserley)

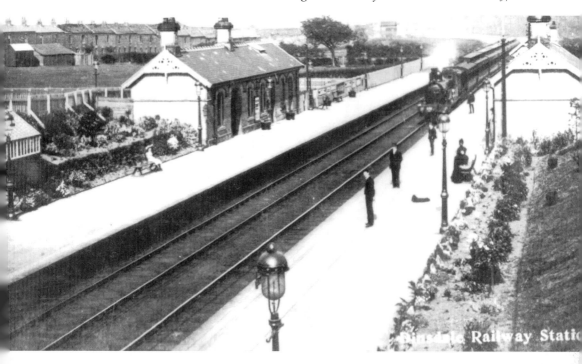

Dinsdale station on the 1887 line from Bank Top to Oak Tree Junction, with a local train approaching. The station here appears to be a simple affair, but the gardens are well kept and would have looked colourful if the picture had been in colour. (LOSA)

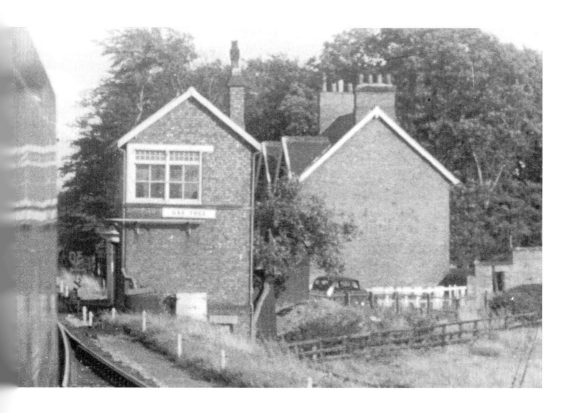

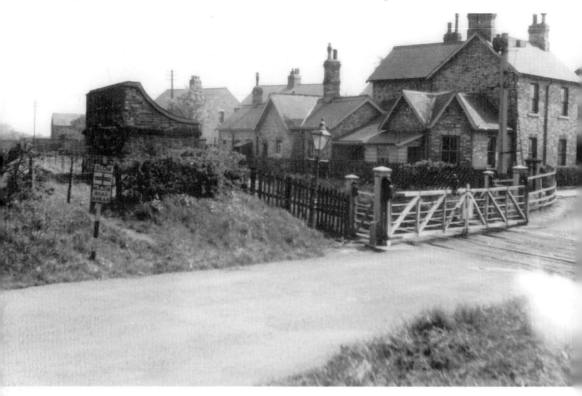

Situated on the old S&DR section between North Road and Oak Tree Junction was the station at Fighting Cocks, closed in 1887, seen here as it appeared in 1949. When the S&DR was first opened, there were no stations as such; the horse-drawn coaches would stop wherever there were passengers to pick up or put down. The usual pick-up points were adjacent to public houses and inns. Indeed, Masons' Arms crossing at Shildon and Fighting Cocks station were both named after local inns where waiting passengers could enjoy refreshments while waiting to travel. Perhaps this is where the idea for refreshment rooms at railway stations across the whole network began. (H. Casserley)

MIDDLESBROUGH, STOCKTON, and WEST HARTLEPOOL (Auto-cars).—North Eastern.

Miles.	Down.	Week Days.							Miles.	Up.	Week Days.					
		mrn	mrn	mrn	aft	aft	aft	aft			mrn	mrn	aft	aft	aft	aft
	Middlesbrougn ......dep.	7 22	9 20	11 0	1 20	3 55	7 30	8 48		West Hartlepool......dep.	8 8	10 20	12 40	2 45	6 30	8 1
5¼	Stockton ....{ arr.	7 34	9 32	11 12	1 32	4 7	7 41	8 58	11½	Stockton ....{ arr.	8 30	10 38	12 58	3 3	6 48	8 2
	{ dep.	7 36	9 34	11 14	1 35	4 9	7 44	9 0		{ dep.	8 31	10 40	1 0	3 5	6 50	8 3
17	West Hartlepool 700 arr.	7 56	9 56	11 34	1 55	4 29	8 6	9 20	17	Middlesbrough ......arr.	8 43	10 52	1 12	3 17	7 2	8 4

☞ For **OTHER TRAINS** between Stockton and West Hartlepool, see pages 708 to 711.

A 1910 timetable for the autocar service between Middlesbrough, Stockton and West Hartlepool. (Author's collection)

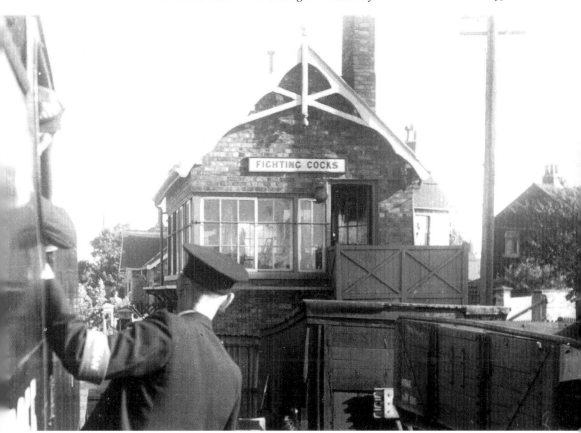

The signal box at Fighting Cocks as it appeared in September 1955. At this time, the line here was freight only, and this appears to be an excursion running over as much of the original S&DR as possible. Between Oak Tree Junction and Stockton-on-Tees, the old S&DR line is still in use as far as Eaglescliffe, and two new stations have been opened at Teesside airport and Allens West, a halt for workmen opened in the Second World War. (R. Casserley)

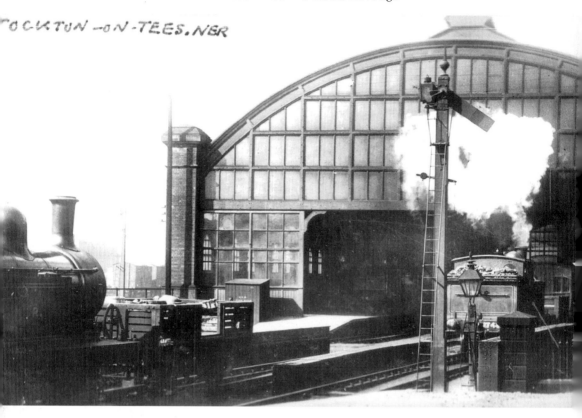

From Allens West, the little branch to Yarm diverged to serve the market town and was worked by horse bus from opening in October 1825 until steam began to work passenger trains in 1833. When steam began to operate, trains only served stations on the main line, and the branch was left to deal with coal traffic until the junction was closed on 16 June 1862. In 1852, the Leeds Northern Railway extended its line from Thirsk to Stockton-on-Tees, via Eaglescliffe, and a new through station was opened in the town some distance north of the S&DR terminus. This station is seen here in NER days, with a tank engine acting as station pilot and a little 0-6-0 engine shunting on the opposite platform. At Eaglescliffe, the original S&DR line was east of the Yarm–Stockton road, and the Leeds Northern line was laid on the west side of the road. For interchange purposes, however, it was decided to allow the LNR to lay tracks alongside their own for use by the S&DR, and the company used the new system from 25 January 1853. (LOSA)

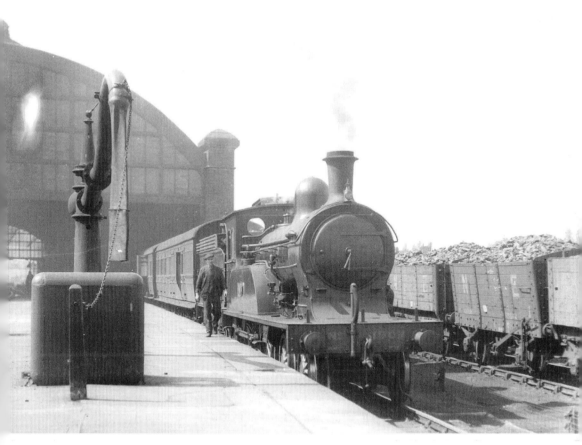

Stockton railway station on 3 June 1935; ex-NER 4-4-0 (LNER Class D17) No. 1907, still in NER livery, has recently arrived with the 8.55 a.m. from Ripon. This through station was originally known as 'North Stockton' to avoid confusion with the S&DR terminus and was developed by the Leeds Northern Railway, Stockton & Hartlepool Railway and Clarence Railway; it probably dates back to 1852. In 1893 the 'North' was dropped from the station name, and it just became 'Stockton'. An accident occurred on 21 July 1852 due to inadequate signalling and the track layout just outside the station. At 5.40 p.m. that afternoon the signalman heard the whistle of a Down train and just before he turned the signal off, he saw a train of trucks standing on the Down line of the Clarence Railway, around 200 yards above the points, the engine being at the far end of the train. The signalman considered that the Down train was 300 yards away before he turned off the signal. As the signal was turned off, the train of wagons shunted down to the points but the signalman thought that the goods train was only coming a little way and intended to stop at the points; when he saw the speed at which shunting was taking place, he turned on the red signal and another signalman tried to stop the goods train but in vain. The front wagon struck the splash plate of the passenger train engine, which caused the wreckage of two or three of the following carriages and killed one passenger. Other incidents occurred over the years, including a derailment on 31 May 1859 at the S&DR station, a boiler explosion on 7 March 1871, a collision of a passenger train with empty carriages at the NER Stockton station on 27 November 1871 due to misrouting of a train, a derailment on 14 August 1873, and a head-on collision at the station on 8 February 1930 that injured two people. (H. Casserley)

NEWCASTLE, LEAMSIDE, FERRYHILL, STOCKTON, and MIDDLESBROUGH.—North Eastern.

Miles	Down.	Week Days.																		Sundays.			
	Central Station,	mrn	mrn	m	mrn	mrn	aft	aft	aft	aft	aft	aft	aft	aft	aft	aft	aft	aft	aft	mrn	mrn	aft	af
	Newcastle ....dep.	5 10	6 50	7 53	8 30	1027	1225	2 7	....	3 25	5 12	5 25	6 45	7 32	7 50	8 5	9 45	1115	Saturdays only.	6 25	8 35	5 20	7 4
¾	Gateshead East	5 13	6 53	7 56	8 33	1030	1228	2 12	....	3 29	5 15	Via Durham.	6 48	Via Durham.	7 54	8 8	9 48	1119		6 30	8 38	5 24	7 4
2¼	Felling	5 18	6 58	8 1	8 38	1035	1233	2 17	....	3 34	5 20		6 53		7 59	8 13	9 53	1124		6 35	8 43	5 29	7
3½	Pelaw	5 22	7 4	8 6	8 43	1040	1238	2 24	....	3 39	5 25		6 58		8 4	8 18	9 58	1129		6 44	8 48	5 34	7
7	Usworth	5 30	7 12	8 14	8 51	1048	1246	2 31	....	3 48	5 32		7 6		8 13	8 26	10 6	1136		6 52	8 56	5 42	8
8¾	Washington	5 34	7 16	8 18	8 55	1052	1250	2 35	....	3 54	5 36		7 11		8 19	8 30	1011	1140		6 57	9 0	5 47	8
10	Penshaw **701**	5 39	7 21	8 24	9 0	1057	1256	2 40	....	4 0	5 41		7 17		8 25	8 35	1017	1146		7 2	9 5	5 52	8
12	Fencehouses	5 46	7 26	8 31	9 6	11 2	1 1	2 45	....	4 6	5 46		....		8 31	8 40	1022	1152		7 8	9 10	5 58	8
14½	Leamside **701**.... arr.	5 53	7 32	8 38	9 12	11 8	1 7	2 51	....	4 12	5 52		....		8 38	8 47	1029	1158		7 15	9 16	6 5	8
	Leamside **701**.... dep.	6 3	7 51	8 39	9 15	1113	1 8	2 52	....	4 15	5 53		....		8 39	8 49	....	Wednesdays and Saturdays.	1159	7 19	9 20	6 9	8
17	Sherburn Colliery	6 10	7 58	To Durham, see page 701.	9 22	1120	To Durham, see page 701.	2 59	....	4 22	5 59		....		On 9th and 23rd inst. To Durham, see page 701.	8 56	....		12 6	7 26	To Durham, see page 701.	6 16	8
19¾	Shincliffe	6 16	8 4		9 28	1126		3 5	....	4 29	6 5		....			9 2	....		1212	7 32		6 22	8
23¾	**Ferryhill 686, 704** arr.	6 25	8 15		9 37	1137		3 14	....	4 39	6 13	6 30	....	8 34		9 11	....		1220	7 41		6 31	8
36½	**686** Darlington (B.T.) a	....	9 6		10 2	1221		4 36	....	5 12	6 37	7 37	....	....		....	....		....	8 16		7 6	..
80¾	**686** York .... "	....	1056		1128	1 52		6 10	....	6 36	8 34	9 18	....	....		.. .	....		....	1016		9 0	..
—	**Ferryhill** ....dep.	6 35	8 36		9 45	1157		3 28	4 37	....	....	6 40	....	8 37		9c15	....		....	....		....	..
26¾	Sedgefield	6 42	8 44		9 52	12 4		3 35	4 44	....	....	6 47	....	8 44		9c23	....		....	....		....	..
31¼	Stillington	6 50	8 52		10 0	1212		3 43	4 52	....	....	6 55	....	8 52		9c32	....		....	....		....	..
33	Carlton	6 54	8 56		10 3	1216		3 47	4 56	....	....	6 59	....	8 56		9c37	....		....	....		....	..
37	Stockton **706, 708, 710, 712** arr.	7 4	9 7		1014	1228		3 58	5 7	....	....	7 11	....	9 8		9c50	....		....	....		....	..
	Stockton dep.	7 10	9 10	....	1016	1232	....	4 15	5 40	....	....	7 17	....	9 14		9c52	....		....	....		....	..
39½	Thornaby	7 16	9 16	....	1022	1238	....	4 22	5 46	....	....	7 23	....	9 20		9c58	....		....	....		....	..
41¼	Newport	....	9 21	....	....	1243	....	....	....	....	....	7 28	....	....		....	....		....	....		....	..
42	**Middlesbrough 706** arr.	7 22	9 25	....	1030	1247	....	4 28	5 52	....	....	7 32	....	9 26		10c4	....		....	....		....	..

Miles	Up.	Week Days.																		Sundays.			
		mrn	mrn	mrn	mrn	mrn	aft	aft	aft	aft	aft	aft	aft	aft	aft	aft	aft			mrn	aft	aft	a
	Middlesbrough....dep.	....	7 13	8 45	Runs on 9th and 23rd instant.	9 25	....	1 29	3 8	....	5 44	....	7 45	....	....	....	1035	....	....	....	From West Hartlepool, see page 704.	....	..
¾	Newport	....	....	....		....	....	....	3 12	....	....	....	7 49	....	....	Saturdays only.	....	....	....	....		....	..
2¾	Thornaby	....	7 19	8 51		9 31	....	1 35	3 17	....	5 50	....	7 54	....	....		1041	....	....	....		....	..
5	Stockton **708, 712** arr.	....	7 27	8 59		9 39	From Durham, see page 701.	1 43	3 25	From Durham, see page 701.	5 58	....	8 1	Saturdays only.	Except Saturdays.		1050	....	....	....		....	..
	Stockton dep.	....	7 31	9 1		9 43		1 48	3 30		6 26	....	8 22				1054	....	....	....		....	..
9	Carlton	....	7 41	....		9 54		1 58	3 40		6 36	....	8 32				11 4	....	....	....		....	..
10¾	Stillington	....	7 47	....		9 59		2 3	3 45		6 41	....	8 37				11 9	....	....	....		....	..
15¼	Sedgefield	....	7 57	....		10 9		2 13	3 55		6 51	....	8 47				1119	....	....	....		....	..
18¾	**Ferryhill 684, 704** arr.	....	8 6	9 25		1017		2 23	4 4		7 0	....	8 56				1127	....	....	....		....	..
—	**684** York ....dep.	3 45	5 55	....		7 40		1250	....		4 55	....	....			9 13	Wednesdays and Saturdays.	....	....	6 30		....	6
—	**684** Darlington (B.T.) "	4 51	7 52	....		9 5		1 57	....		6 33	....	....			10 8		....	....	8 20		7 35	8
—	**Ferryhill** ....dep.	7 35	8 30	....		1023		2 33	....		7 12	....	....			1037		....	....	8 50	6 1	8 6	8
22¾	Shincliffe	7 46	8 41	....		1034		2 44	....		7 23	....	....			1047		....	....	9 0	6 11	8 16	
25	Sherburn Colliery	7 52	8 47	....		1040		2 50	....		7 29	....	....			1053		....	....	9 6	6 17	8 23	
27½	Leamside **701**.... arr.	7 58	8 54	....		1046	1 39	2 56	....	5 32	7 35	....	....			1059		....	....	9 12	6 23	8 30	8
	Leamside **701**.... dep.	8 3	9 2	....	1035	1047	1 40	2 57	....	5 33	7 47	....	....	1015	1051	11 3		....	....	9 15	6 25	8 33	8
30	Fencehouses	8 8	9 7	....	1041	1053	1 46	3 3	....	5 39	7 52	....	....	1020	1057	11 9		....	....	9 21	6 31	8 39	9
32	Penshaw **701**	8 13	9 12	....	1046	1058	1 51	3 8	....	5 44	7 57	9 0	....	1026	11 2	1115		....	....	9 27	6 37	8 45	9
33¾	Washington	8 18	9 16	....	1051	11 3	1 55	3 14	....	5 48	8 3	9 6	....	1031	11 7	1121		....	....	9 33	6 43	8 51	9
35	Usworth	8 22	9 20	....	1056	11 8	1 59	3 19	....	5 52	8 8	9 11	....	1035	1111	1126		....	....	9 38	6 48	8 56	9
38½	Pelaw	8 29	9 26	....	11 3	1116	2 6	3 27	....	5 59	8 16	9 18	....	1042	1118	1137		....	....	9 47	6 56	9 5	9
39¾	Felling	8 33	9 30	....	11 7	1120	2 10	3 31	....	6 3	8 20	9 22	....	....	1122	1141		....	....	9 52	7 0	9 9	9
41½	Gateshead East [to **698**	8 40	9 36	....	1114	1126	2 16	3 37	....	6 9	8 26	9 29	....	....	1128	1147		....	....	10 0	7 7	9 18	9
42	**Newcastle** (Cen) **690** arr.	8 43	9 39	....	1117	1129	2 20	3 40	....	6 12	8 29	9 34	....	....	11 31	1150		....	....	10 3	7 10	9 21	9

b Stops when required to set down from beyond Darlington. *c* Wednesdays and Saturdays. **m** Auto-car.

For **OTHER TRAINS** between Newcastle and Pelaw, see pages 692 and 693; between Penshaw and Leamside, see page 701.

An NER timetable for services which served Stockton from Newcastle, Ferryhill and Middlesbrough. (Author's collection)

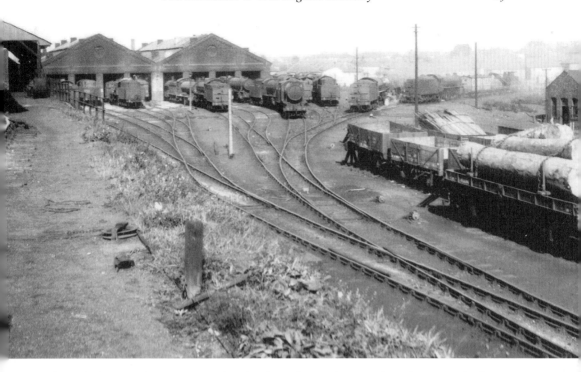

The loco shed at Stockton in 1949, shortly after takeover by British Railways, with plenty of locos in view. A loco shed was completed with the Leeds Northern line in 1852 and, a decade later, increased accommodation was required so the shed was doubled in size at a cost of £1093 10s 6d. This was a six-road shed immediately west of the station. In 1889, a new site was sought for a shed and, in October, plans were submitted, at a cost of £16,500, for a shed to hold twenty-four engines. A tender for £12,099 7s 7d was accepted on 14 November, but was amended to £12,520 2s 9d the following month. This new shed was completed in 1891 after excess expenditure of £445 10s had been authorised. This single-ended eight-road shed lasted until closure on 13 June 1959. Stockton shed was responsible for both passenger and goods workings, passenger workings being local in nature. In 1939, passenger workings were as follows:

G5 0-4-4T for Port Clarence, West Hartlepool and Battersby.
A8 4-6-2T for West Hartlepool, Thirsk and Whitby.
A8 4-6-2T for Harrogate, Darlington and West Hartlepool.
A8 4-6-2T for Port Clarence and Ferryhill.
Sentinel Railcars served
1) Pelaw, Newcastle, Ferryhill, Whitby and Goathland.
2) Port Clarence, Battersby, Guisborough and Ferryhill.
3) Port Clarence and Ferryhill.

During the summer months, Stockton shed was also responsible for some workings along the Yorkshire coast to Scarborough, using A5, A6 and A8 4-6-2Ts, L1 2-6-4Ts and, in the 1950s, LMR 2-6-0s.

In 1930 Stockton's allocation was reduced from forty-seven to nineteen locos due to closure of Stockton marshalling yards. However, the yards reopened during the Second World War to handle increased freight traffic, and, by 1947, the shed had a larger allocation than in 1923. After the war, the shed became responsible for a number of braked freight trains, mostly to York, and to cover this traffic, eleven B1 4-6-0s were allocated to the shed.

In 1949, the allocation was as follows:

BR Code 51E.

B1 4-6-0	61017 *Bushbuck.*
B1 4-6-0	61018 *Gnu.*
B1 4-6-0	61030 *Nyala.*
B1 4-6-0	61032 *Stembock.*
B1 4-6-0	61034 *Chiru.*
B1 4-6-0	61037 *Jairou.*
B1 4-6-0	61189 *Sir William Gray.*
B1 4-6-0	61213, 61220, 61290, 61303.
K1 2-6-0	62041, 62042, 62043.
Q6 0-8-0	63349, 63369, 63380, 63393, 63459.
J25 0-6-0	65689, 65781.
J27 0-6-0	65860, 65868, 65887.
G5 0-4-4T	67242, 67278, 67288, 67305, 67317, 67318.
Y1 Sentinel 0-4-0T	68144.
J71 0-6-0T	68305.
J77 0-6-0T	68407, 68412, 68420.
A7 4-6-2T	69781, 69787.
T1 4-8-0T	69918.
WD/O7 2-8-0	90012, 90048, 90067, 90082, 90086, 90092, 90155, 90172, 90184, 90240, 90344, 90377, 90405, 90603, 90623.

Total: 53. (H. Casserley)

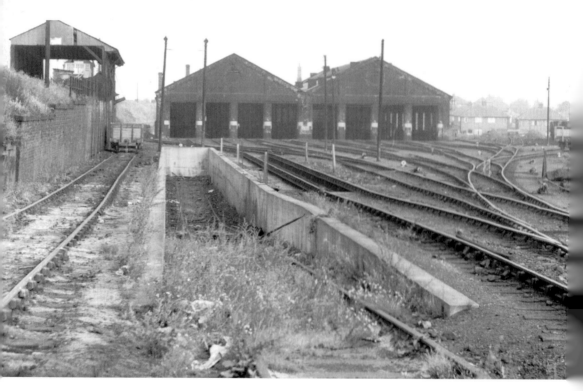

On 30 August 1959, Stockton loco shed remains standing, but without an allocation, following closure the previous year. (R. Carpenter)

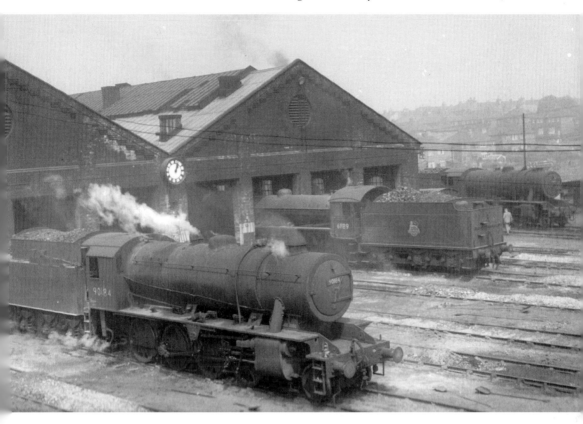

Stockton loco shed on 17 May 1952, showing examples of ex-WD 2-8-0 engines, including No. 90184 in the foreground. Also, in the middle background is ex-LNER Thompson B1 4-6-0 No. 61189 *Sir William Gray*. The shed was closed in 1959, the allocation going to the new shed at Thornaby. After the shed was closed, it stood empty for a while until taken over by a private company. At closure the final allocation was as follows:

B1 4-6-0	61030 *Nyala*.
B1 4-6-0	61032 *Sembock*.
B1 4-6-0	61034 *Chiru*.
B1 4-6-0	61173, 61220, 61303.
K1 2-6-0	62001, 62003, 62041, 62042, 62047, 62065.
J26 0-6-0	65747, 65773.
J27 0-6-0	65787, 65788, 65853, 65854.
L1 2-6-4T	67754, 67766.
J94 0-6-0ST	68049.
J71 0-6-0T	68260
J72 0-6-0T	68696.
J50 0-6-0T	68892.
LMR 2MT 2-6-0	46478.
WD 2-8-0	90082, 90155, 90172, 90184, 90377, 90430.

Total: 31. (H. Casserley)

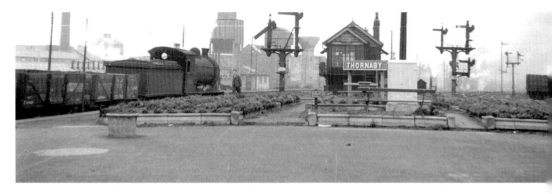

Thornaby station on 27 April 1954, looking towards Newport, which had a station called Port Darlington from December 1830 and a coal staithe dock facility. So successful was the port that it was overwhelmed by the volume of traffic, and work started on what would become a new port at Middlesbrough in 1839. As Middlesbrough developed, extra railway facilities were required for the increasing numbers of goods wagons needed for the docks. Thus, in 1882, the NER built South Stockton railway station, which was opened in October. In 1892, however, a charter was granted that created the Borough of Thornaby-on-Tees, which incorporated the village of Thornaby and South Stockton, so, on 1 November, the station name was changed to Thornaby. Passing through Thornaby station at this time is ex-LNER Class J26 0-6-0, No. 65734, with a goods train heading for Middlesbrough docks. The station is in the middle of major industry, as can be seen in the background. (H. Casserley)

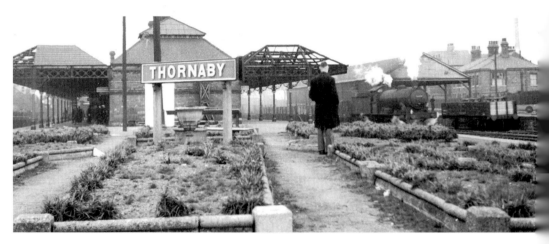

Another view of Thornaby station, looking back towards Eaglescliffe with another ex-LNER loco, this time a Q6 0-8-0, No. 63442, with a goods train heading for the docks. After takeover by BR, the very smart station had become rather dilapidated and lacked repair, but station staff maintained well-kept flower borders. As passenger numbers fell, the station continued to decline and vandalism was rampant so, despite local protests, the building was demolished in December 1981. The fortunes of the station improved when Durham University developed its Queen's Campus, and a Transpennine Express service to Manchester airport was commenced early in the twenty-first century. The newly refurbished station was reopened on 7 February 2003. Thornaby had a new motive power depot opened in 1958, coded 51L, and locos were transferred from Middlesbrough and Newport, followed a year later, in June 1959, by those from Stockton and Haverton Hill. Thornaby MPD was part of BR's project to centralise all marshalling yards in the West Auckland and Middlesbrough areas into one yard. The depot here survived until closure in the last year. (H. Casserley)

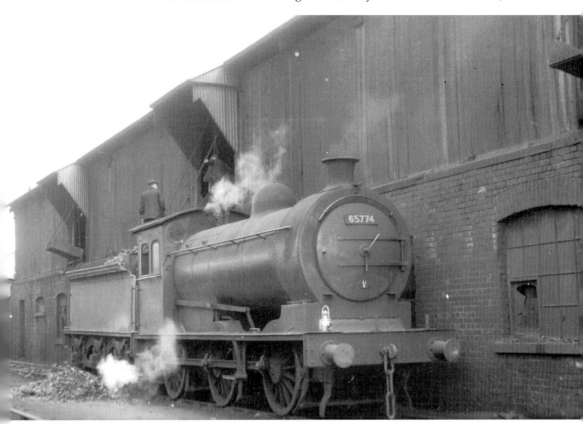

Exterior of Newport loco shed on 17 May 1952 with ex-NER and LNER Class J27 0-6-0 No. 65774 being coaled. This freight shed was situated in the middle of Newport marshalling yards between Middlesbrough and Thornaby. In the summer, however, its allocation of J39 0-6-0 engines was often used on passenger trains to the coast. From February 1943, the shed was given an allocation of six passenger engines – D17/1 4-4-0 No. 1629 and D20 4-4-0s Nos 1026, 1184, 1209, 1232 and 1672 – but these were used to assist heavy trains up the 3-mile 1 in 170 bank between Yarm and Picton, on the Leeds Northern line, en route to Northallerton. The normal allocation was usually six and eight coupled engines. Between November 1943 and October 1944, forty-seven WD 2-8-0s arrived at Newport but were returned to the War Department between December 1944 and February 1945. After the war, the class returned to Newport from November 1945, with twenty-four being allocated by the end of the year.

In June 1880, an estimate of £8,850 was given for a loco shed with extra deep foundations, plus another £1,813 for a coal stage (seen in this view), all of which were authorised on 15 July 1880. Despite the deep foundations, the shed became unsafe due to subsidence, and on 31 May 1888 it was recommended that a new shed be built on a different site. The cost of rebuilding the old shed and constructing a new one was estimated to be £13,250, and was completed in November 1890, costing £394 more than estimated. The 1890 building consisted of two turntables and their associated staff under one roof, but in November 1901 extra sidings were required at an estimated cost of £350. During the Second World War, a lightly constructed straight shed was built adjacent to the east wall of the main building to facilitate much needed repair space for locos. In the 1930s the main building was allowed to deteriorate into a bad state of repair due to neglect and the state of the economy at that time, culminating in the collapse of part of the roof in January 1939, which killed the foreman cleaner. (H. Casserley)

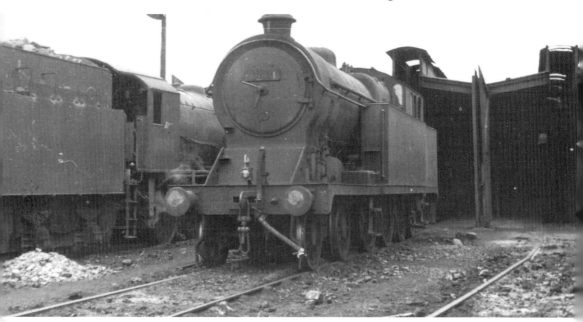

Standing outside Newport shed on 27 April 1954 is ex-LNER Class A5/2 4-6-2T No. 69831 ,alongside an unidentified ex-WD 2-8-0. The shed here looks in a poor state of repair. A year after coming into BR ownership, the allocation for 1949 was as follows:

BR code 51B.

Q5 0-8-0	63274.
Q6 0-8-0	63341, 63343, 63344, 63345, 63347, 63360, 63370, 63371, 63388, 63389, 63426, 63430, 63445, 63447.
J24 0-6-0	65601, 65604.
J26 0-6-0	65730, 65731, 65732, 65734, 65735, 65736, 65737, 65738, 65739, 65740, 65741, 65742, 65743, 65744, 65745, 65746, 65749, 65750, 65751, 65752, 65753, 65754, 65755, 65756, 65757, 65758, 65759, 65760, 65761, 65762, 65763, 65765, 65766, 65767, 65768, 65769, 65770, 65772, 65773, 65774, 65777, 65778.
J94 0-6-0ST	68007, 68011, 68023 68037, 68049, 68060, 68062.
T1 4-8-0T	69910, 69911, 69913, 69916, 69917, 69919, 69921.
WD 2-8-0	90014, 90016, 90027, 90045, 90054, 90068, 90074, 90081, 90089, 90090, 90091, 90098, 90132, 90230, 90273, 90373, 90426, 90434, 90446, 90451, 90452, 90457, 90459, 90461, 90462, 90465, 90467, 90475, 90481, 90487, 90488, 90500, 90517, 90605, 90625.

Total: 108.

When the new MPD opened at Thornaby, all Newport locos were transferred there on 1 June 1958, and the buildings were demolished to make way for the new Tees marshalling yard. When the branch to Middlesbrough was opened, there was a passenger station at Newport, but it was closed in 1915 as a wartime measure, and never reopened. (H. Casserley)

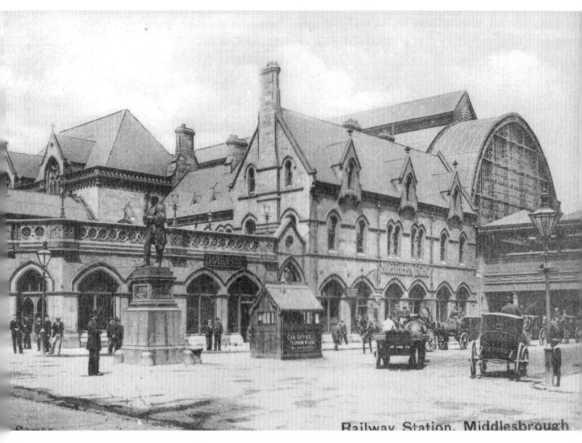

The very elegant terminus station at Middlesbrough as it appeared early in the twentieth century, with horse-drawn carriages in the concourse. This is the last station, built in 1877. It was designed by North Eastern Railway Chief Architect William Peachey, and had an ornate Gothic frontage with an overall roof, of elliptical design, which was constructed of wrought iron to a lattice design. This roof had glass covering the centre, with timber on the inside and slate on the outside. The two end screens were glazed, with timber cladding around the outer edges. The station had a very high roof in relation to its width, and was destroyed in a German daylight air raid in the afternoon of 3 August 1942. (LOSA)

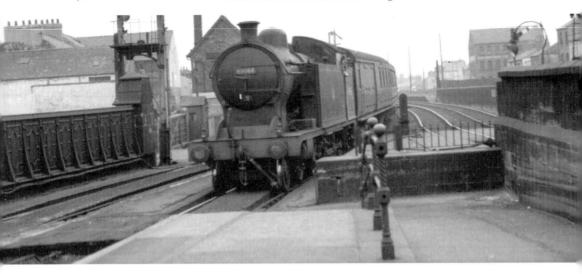

Arriving at Middlesbrough station on 27 April 1954 is ex-LNER Class A8 4-6-2T No. 69866, with a train from Whitby. (H. Casserley)

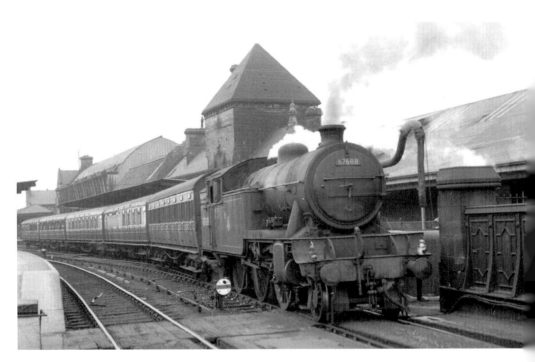

Middlesbrough station in 1954, with ex-LNER Class V3 2-6-2T No. 67688 about to depart with a local train. Note that the overall roof has disappeared as a result of enemy action during the Second World War. (H. Casserley)

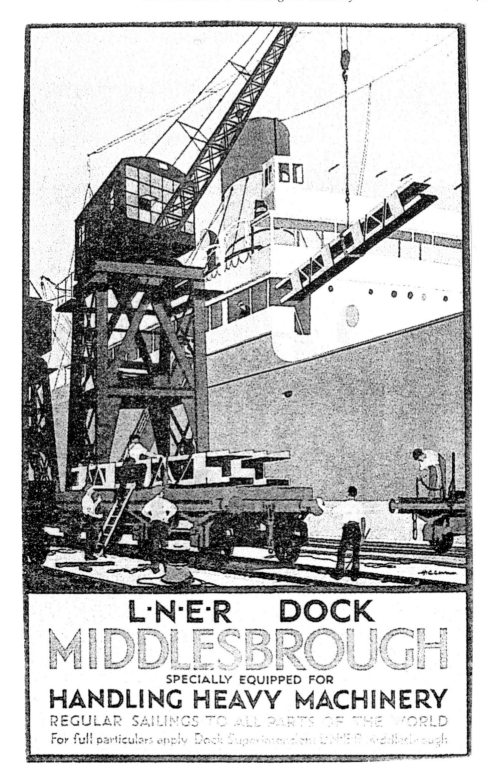

An advertisement of 1927 by the LNER for the docks at Middlesbrough, making the point that the port could handle heavy machinery. (Author's collection)

NEWCASTLE, SEAHAM, WEST HARTLEPOOL, and MIDDLESBROUGH.—North Eastern.

Miles	Down. Week Days.	mrn	mrn	mrn	mrn	mrn	mrn	mrn (Thro' Train, Newcastle to Manchester (Ex.) and Liverpool (Lime St.) see pages 731, 753, 751, 490.)	mrn	mrn	aft (Except Sats.)	mrn (Sats. only.)	aft (Sats. only.)	aft	aft	aft (Sats. only.)	aft (Through Train to Saltburn, see page 756)	aft	aft	aft	aft
	Newcastle (Cen.) dep.	5 5	...	6 25	7 2	8 17	9 17	10 0	...	1117	...	1147	1230	1230	1 17	...	2 17	...	...	3 17	4 17
¼	Gateshead East "	5 8	...	6 28	7 6	8 20	9 20	...	...	1120	...	1150	1234	1234	1 20	...	2 20	...	...	3 20	4 20
12¼	Sunderland "	5 40	...	7 8	8 4	8 42	9 42	1022	1032	1142	12 6	1223	1257	1 15	1 42	2 15	2 42	2 55	3 15	3 42	4 42
15¼	Ryhope East	5 47		...	8 11	...	...	...	1039	...	1213	1230	1 4	1 22	...	2 22	...	3 2	3 22	...	...
17½	Seaham Colliery	5 54	6 10	...	8 17	8 52	9 52	...	1045	...	1219	1236	1 12	1 29	...	2 29	...	3 9	3 28	...	...
17¾	Seaham arr.	5 56	...	...	...	...	...	...	...	...	1221	1238	1 14	...	...	...	...	3 11	...	...	...
21½	Easington	...	6 19	...	8 26	...	...	...	1054	...				1 39	...	2 38	...	...	3 39	...	...
23½	Horden	...	6 24	...	8 32	...	...	...	1059	...				1 45	...	2 43	...	...	3 46	...	...
—	Blackhall Rocks	...	6 29	...	8 37	...	...	...	11 4	...				1 50	...	2 48	...	...	3 51	...	...
30¼	West Hartlepool arr.	...	6 39	7 37	8 47	9 11	1011	1051	1114	1211				2 1	2 11	2 58	3 11	...	4 1	4 11	5 11
41¾	Stockton "	...	7 25	8 5	...	9 37	1034	1113	1149	1233				...	2 32	...	3 33	...	...	4 32	5 33
46¾	Middlesbrough "	...	7 59	8 47	...	9 52	1049	1137	...	1247				...	2 47	...	3 47	...	...	4 47	5 52

Down. Week Days—*Continued.* / Sundays.	aft	aft (Through Train to Saltburn, see page 756)	aft	aft	aft	aft	aft	aft	aft (Weds. & Sats.)	aft (Saturdays only)	Sun. mrn	Sun. mrn	Sun. mrn	Sun. aft	Sun. aft	Sun. aft	Sun. aft
Newcastle (Central) dep.	...	5 17	5 30	5 47	7 17	...	7 47	8 47	9 50	...	...	7 15	...	1227	3 30	5 30	8 30
Gateshead East "	...	5 20	5 33	5 50	7 20	...	7 50	8 50	9 53	...	...	7 18	...	1230	3 33	5 33	8 33
Sunderland "	4 52	5 42	6 5	7 15	7 42	7 55	9 10	9 40	1032	1050	7 35	9 16	1125	3 0	4 55	8 30	9 15
Ryhope East	4 59	...	6 12	7 22	...	8 2	9 17	9 47	1039	1057	...	9 23	1132	3 7	5 2	8 37	9 23
Seaham Colliery	5 6	5 53	6 19	7 28	...	8 9	9 24	9 54	1046	11 4	7 46	9 30	1139	3 14	5 9	8 44	9 30
Seaham arr.	5 8	...	...	7 30	...	...	9 26	...	1048	...	7 48	...	1141	3 16	5 11	8 46	...
Easington	...	...	6 30	...	...	8 19	...	10 3		1113	...	9 39	...	...	...	...	9 40
Horden	...	...	6 37	...	...	8 25	...	10 9		1119	...	9 44	...	...	...	...	9 46
Blackhall Rocks	...	...	6 43	...	...	8 30	...	1014		1124	...	9 49	...	...	...	...	9 51
West Hartlepool arr.	...	6 13	6 54	...	8 11	8 40	...	1024		1134	...	9 59	...	...	...	...	10 1
Stockton "	...	6 34	...	...	8 33	9 24	...	...		...	...	...	...	...	...	...	...
Middlesborough "	...	6 49	...	...	8 48	...	...	...		...	...	...	...	...	...	...	...

Miles	Up. Week Days.	mrn (Except Mons.)	mrn	mrn	mrn	mrn (Through Train from Saltburn, see page 757)	mrn	mrn	mrn	mrn	mrn	aft	mrn (Sats. only.)	aft (Through Train, Liverpool (Lime St.) and Manchester (Ex.) to Newcastle, see pages 486, 751, 752, and 728. Restaurant Car.)	aft (Sats. only.)	aft	aft (Through Train from Saltburn, see page 757)	aft	aft	aft	aft	aft
	Middlesbrough dep.	...	...	...	7 25	8 20	9 20	...	1020	...	1120	...	...	1210	...	...	2 20	...	3 20	...	4 20	...
5	Stockton "	5 17	...	...	7 37	8 33	9 33	9 49	1033	1041	1133	...	1145	1 4	...	...	2 33	...	3 33	...	4 33	...
16½	West Hartlepool "	5 40	...	6 33	8 10	8 57	9 57	1012	1057	1127	1157	...	1240	1 25	...	1 55	2 57	...	3 57	4 25	4 57	...
—	Blackhall Rocks		...	...	8 22	...	...	1024	...	1139	...	...	1254	...	...	2 7	...	...	...	4 37	...	...
23¼	Horden		...	6 47	8 27	...	...	1029	...	1144	...	...	1 1	...	...	2 14	...	...	...	4 42	...	...
25¼	Easington		...	6 52	8 32	...	...	1034	...	1149	...	...	1 8	...	...	2 21	...	...	...	4 47	...	...
—	Seaham dep.		6 18	...	...	...	...	...	...	...	...	1 10	...	...	2 18	...	...	3 42	...	...	...	5 20
29¼	Seaham Colliery		6 20	7 1	8 41	9 18	...	1043	...	1158	...	1 12	1 18	...	2 20	2 31	3 18	3 44	...	4 56	...	5 22
31½	Ryhope East		6 26	7 7	8 47	...	...	1049	...	12 4	...	1 18	1 24	...	2 26	2 37	...	3 50	...	5 2	...	5 28
34½	Sunderland 742 arr.	6 12	6 32	7 13	8 53	9 26	1026	1055	1126	1210	1226	1 25	1 30	1 53	2 32	2 43	3 28	3 56	4 26	5 8	5 26	5 34
46½	Gateshead East "	...	...	8 9	9 32	9 49	1049	1132	1150	...	1249	2 8	2 8	...	...	3 32	3 50	4 32	4 49	5 47	5 51	6 32
46¾	Newcastle (Central) "	6 42	...	8 12	9 35	9 52	1052	1135	1154	...	1252	2 11	2 11	2 23	...	3 35	3 54	4 35	4 52	5 50	5 54	6 35

Up. Week Days—*Continued.* / Sundays.	aft (Thro' Train, Liverpool (Lime St.) & Manchester (Ex.) to Newcastle, see pages 487, 751, 752, & 729.)	aft	aft (Saturdays only.)	aft (Weds. & Sats.)	aft	aft (Saturdays only.)	aft (A Via Eaglescliffe.)	Sun. mrn	Sun. mrn	Sun. mrn	Sun. aft	Sun. aft	Sun. aft	Sun. aft	Sun. aft
Middlesborough dep.	5 51	...	6 45	...	7 45	...	9A54	...	...	...	...	...	...	...	...
Stockton "	6 33	...	7 18	...	8 11	9 40	1045	5 17	...	...	...	...	...	...	...
West Hartlepool "	6 57	...	8 10	...	9 25	1025	11 6	5 43	7 27	...	...	...	...	7 8	...
Blackhall Rocks	...	...	8 22	...	9 37	1037	...	...	7 39	...	...	...	...	7 20	...
Horden	...	...	8 27	...	9 42	1042	...	...	7 44	...	...	...	...	7 25	...
Easington	...	...	8 32	...	9 47	1047	...	...	7 49	...	...	...	...	7 31	...
Seaham dep.	...	8 32	...	9 35	...	...	...	...	...	8 5	1230	3 40	5 18	...	9 0
Seaham Colliery	...	8 35	8 41	9 37	9 56	1056	...	...	7 58	8 7	1232	3 42	5 20	7 41	9 2
Ryhope East	...	8 41	8 47	9 43	10 3	11 2	...	...	8 4	8 13	1238	3 48	5 26	7 47	9 8
Sunderland 742 arr.	7 26	8 47	8 53	9 49	10 9	11 8	1134	6 11	8 10	8 19	1244	3 54	5 32	7 53	9 14
Gateshead East "	7 53	9 57	9 57	...	11 7	...	...	...	...	9 17	1 47	4 43	6 28	9 3	9 58
Newcastle (Central) "	7 57	10 0	10 0	...	1110	...	...	6 37	...	9 20	1 50	4 46	6 31	9 6	10 [illegible]

☞ For **LOCAL TRAINS** and **intermediate Stations** between Newcastle and Sunderland, see page 741; between West Hartlepool, Stockton, and Middlesbrough, see page 755.

⁎ For **OTHER TRAINS** between Newcastle, Sunderland, West Hartlepool, and Stockton, see p. 740; Newcastle and Middlesbrough, see

A 1910 timetable for passenger services between Middlesbrough, West Hartlepool and Newcastle. (Author's collection)

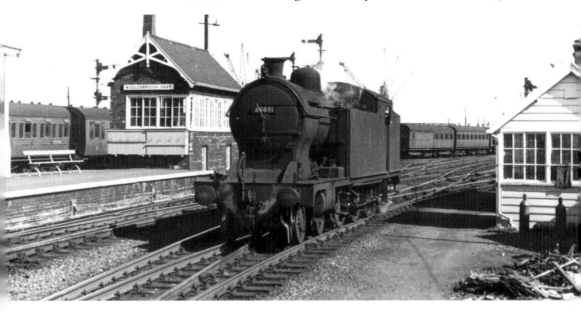

Resting opposite Middlesbrough East signal box on 1 September 1956 as she waits for her next turn of duty is ex-LNER Class A8 4-6-2T No. 69881. Middlesbrough station was witness to some minor accidents over the years, and a few are mentioned here. On 12 August 1872, there was a derailment of unknown cause, and on 26 February 1875 a boiler explosion occurred at Middlesbrough, a fairly common event at this time. On 20 March 1899, a passenger train collided with crossing gates due to greasy rails, and on 20 January 1927, under LNER auspices, there was a sidelong collision; luckily, there were no casualties. (H. Casserley)

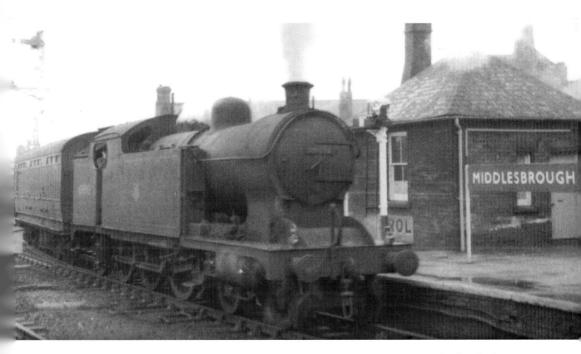

Arriving at Middlesbrough station in 1961 is ex-LNER Class A8 No. 69892 at the head of a train from Saltburn. (R. Carpenter).

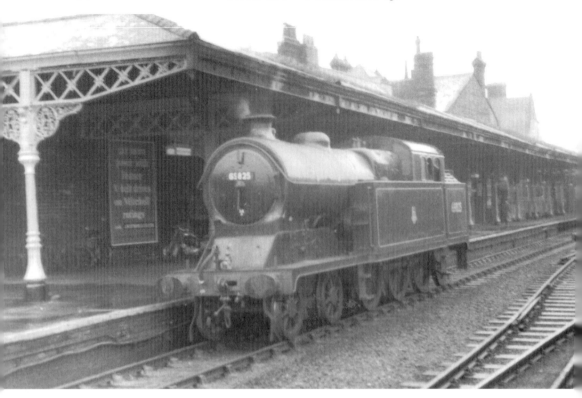

Middlesbrough station in 1961, with ex-LNER Class A5/1 4-6-2T No. 69825 waiting for her turn of duty. These A5/1 Class engines were originally built by Robinson for the Great Central Railway. (R. Carpenter)

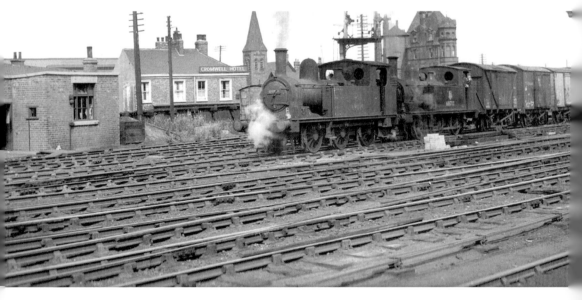

A pair of Class J72 0-6-0Ts, Nos 69019 and 68721, are leaving Middlesbrough docks with a freight train for Newport marshalling yard on 27 July 1955. (R. Carpenter collection)

NEWCASTLE, LEAMSIDE, FERRYHILL, STOCKTON, and MIDDLESBROUGH.—North Eastern.

Down.

				Week Days.													Sundays.	
	mrn	mrn	mrn	mrn	mrn	aft	aft	aft	aft	aft	aft	aft	aft	aft			mrn	aft
Newcastle (Cen.) ..dep.	4 55	6 56	8 35	....	1015	1225	1 35	....	2 42	....	5 7	7 5	5 8 53	1035	....		6 18	5 12
Gateshead East	4 58	7 0	8 38	....	1018	1228	1 38	....	2 52	....	5 10	7 8	7 58 8 57	1038	....		6 23	5 16
Felling	5 3	7 5	8 43	....	1023	1233	1 43	....	2 56	....	....	7 13	8 3 9	2 1043	....		6 28	5 21
Pelaw	5 9	7 10	8 47	....	1027	1238	1 47	....	3 5	....	5 18	7 17	8 7 9	7 1047	....		6 37	5 26
Usworth	5 17	7 20	8 55	....	1035	1246	1 56	....	3 12	....	5 26	7 25	8 15 9 16	1055	....		6 46	5 34
Washington	5 21	7A32	8 59	....	1039	1250	2 1	....	3 17	....	5 31	7 30	8 19 9 21	1059	....		6 51	5 39
Penshaw 742	5 26	7 38	9 4	....	1044	1256	2 6	....		....	5 37	7 36	8 24 9 27	11 4	....		6 56	5 44
Fencehouses	5 32	7 44	9 12	....	1051	1	2 15	....		....	5 42	7 42	8 31 9 34	1110	....		7 3	5 52
Leamside 742.... { arr.	5 38	7 50	9 18	....	1057	1 8	2 21	....		....	5 48	7 48	8 37 9 40	1116	....		7 9	5 58
{ dep.	5 55	7 53	9 21	....	11 9		2 24	....		....	5 51		8 43		....		7 15	6 9
Sherburn Colliery	....	7 59	9 28	....	1117		2 30	....		....	5 57		8 50		....		7 22	6 16
Shincliffe	....	8 5	9 34	....	1124		2 36	....		....	6 3		8 56		....		7 28	6 23
Ferryhill **731**, 742arr.	6 13	8 15	9 42	....	1135		2 46	....		....	6 11		9 6		....		7 37	6 33
731 DARLINGTON *. arr.	....	9 9	1053	....	1221		3 21	....		....	6 41				....		8 10	7 7
731 YORK......... "	....	1134	1210	....	2 14		4 48	....		....	8 30				....		10 6	9 5
731 NEWCASTLE ....dep.	....	7 5		....	1035			1 58	3 40	5 15	....				....		7 30	
Ferryhill ....dep.	6 35	8 36		....	9 47	1156		3 28	4 42	7 10	....				....		9 20	
Sedgefield	6 42	8 44		....	9 54	12 3		3 35	4 49	7 17	....				....		9 28	
Stillington	6 50	8 52		....	10 2	1211		3 43	4 57	7 26	....				....		9 37	
Carlton 1764	....	8 56		....	10 6	1215		3 47	5 1	7 32	....				....		9 42	
Stockton 753, 755 arr.	7 4	9 7		....	1017	1229		4 0	5 12	7 40	....				....		9 55	
Midd!esbrough 756 "	7 22	9 22		....	1033	1247		4 23	5 52	7 55	....				....			

Up.

					Week Days.											Sundays.	
	mrn		mrn	mrn		mrn	aft	aft	aft	aft	aft		aft	aft	aft	mrn	aft
Middlesbrough....dep.	....		7 10	8 45	....	9 20		1210	....	3 8		5 51	....	7 45	....		1015
Stockton............ "	....		7 28	9 1	....	9 43		1 40	....	3 28		6 15	....	8 25	....		1025
Carlton	....		7 38		....	9 54		1 50	....	3 38		6 25	....	d	....		1030
Stillington	....		7 44	a	....	9 59		1 55	....	3 43		6 30	....	8 40	....		1040
Sedgefield	....		7 54		....	10 9		2 5	....	3 53		6 40	....	8 50	....		1049
Ferryhill **728**, 742arr.	....		8 3	9 28	....	1017		2 15	....	4 2		6 49	....	8 59	....		
728 NEWCASTLE .... arr.	....		9 16	1020	....	1137		3 15	....	5 28		8 26	1033		....		
728 YORK......... dep.	3 50				....	7 5		1250	....			4 47			....		6 30 6 43
728 DARLINGTON *. "	4 55		7 49		....	9 3		2 0	....			6 35			....		8 25 8 6
Ferryhill.........dep.	7 34		8 28		....	1023		2 37	....			7 24	9 5		....		8 56 8 36
Shincliffe	7 45		8 39		....	1034		2 48	....			7 34	9 16		....		9 6 8 46
Sherburn Colliery	7 51		8 45		....	1040		2 54	....			7 40	9 22		....		9 12 8 52
Leamside 742.... { arr.	7 57		8 52		....	1046	12 23	3 0	....			5 38 7 46	9 28		....		9 19 8 58
{ dep.	7 59		8 59		....	1050	1 50	3 1	....			5 39 7 47	9 29		....		9 24 9 4
Fencehouses	8 5		9 5		....	1056	1 56	3 7	....			5 45 7 53	9 35		....		9 30 9 10
Penshaw 742	8 10		9 10		....	11 12	1 3	12 4 27	....			5 50 7 58	9 40		....		9 35 9 15
Washington	8 15		9 15		....	11 6	2 6	3 17 4 32	....			5 55 8 3	9 45		....		9 41 9 21
Usworth	8 20		9 20		....	1111	2 10	3 22 4 37	....			6 0 8 8	9 50		....		9 46 9 26
Pelaw 739, 744	8 28		9 28		....	1118	2 18	3 29 4 46	....			6 7 8 16	9 58		....		9 55 9 37
Felling	8 32		9 32		....	1122	2 22	3 33 4 50	....			6 11 8 20	10 2		....		9 59 9 42
Gateshead East [to 754	8 39		9 40		....	1128	2 30	3 39	....			6 16 8 26	1010		....		10 7 9 49
Newcastle (Cen) 734arr.	8 43		9 43		....	1131	2 33	3 43 5 3	....			6 19 8 29	1013		....		1010 9 52

*Arrives Washington 7 24 mrn. on Saturdays. **a** Stops at Stillington when required to set down. **b** Arrives York 10 53 mrn. on Saturdays. **d** Stops on Saturdays, also on Wednesdays when required to set down. * Bank Top Station.
For **LOCAL TRAINS and intermediate Stations** between Stockton & Middlesbro', page 755.
For **OTHER TRAINS** between Newcastle and Pelaw, pages 739 and 741; Newcastle and Ferryhill, page 731; Newcastle and Middlesbro' page 754; Penshaw and Leamside, page 742.

A 1910 timetable for trains operating between Newcastle and Middlesbrough, via Leamside, Ferryhill and Stockton. (Author's collection)

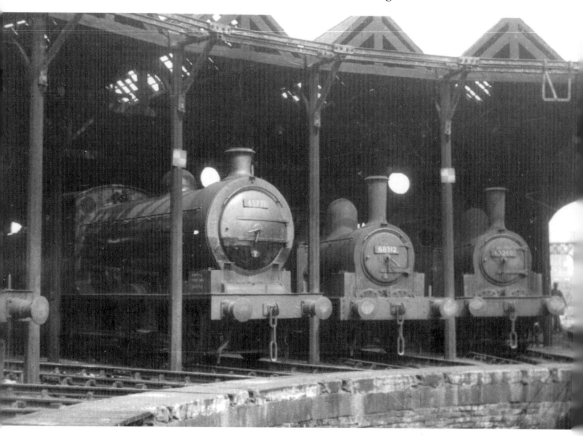

Standing around the turntable at Middlesbrough engine shed on 17 May 1952 are, from left to right, ex-NER and LNER Worsdell Class J26 0-6-0 No. 65771, a larger boiler version of Class J24. Right of the J26 are a pair of ex-NER and LNER Worsdell Class J71 0-6-0Ts, Nos 68312 and 68260. The first reference to a loco shed at Middlesbrough was made in November 1845, when a proposal was made to extend the existing structure. In January 1849, a further shed was authorised 'to be erected nearly opposite to the sail cloth factory', but by 1854, accommodation was still only sufficient for four engines, although six were allocated and a new shed for sixteen engines was started in the same year. Before this shed was completed, it was fitted with gas lighting and benches to allow work to be undertaken on the allocated locos. By 1865, this shed had an allocation of twenty-seven engines. On 22 November 1865, a tender of £4,566 was accepted for a circular shed, followed a few days later by plans for further accommodation, and, on 27 December 1865, a tender was accepted for a second circular shed from Messrs Shaftoe & Barry (who had built the first shed) for £4,500. The sheds were completed in August 1866 and February 1867 respectively, with excess expenditure of £1,478 2s 2d for the first shed and £688 4s 8d for the second. A third roundhouse was authorised in 1870, at an estimated cost of £5,500, completed early in 1872, the cost overrunning by £982 1s 1d. Along with Middlesbrough railway station, the shed also suffered bomb damage during the Second World War, which resulted in the demolition of one of the roundhouses, meaning that the turntable was open to the elements. The remaining two roundhouses stayed in use until the shed closed on 31 May 1958, becoming more ramshackle as the years went by, as can be seen in this view. The shed was finally demolished between 1959 and 1960. (H. Casserley)

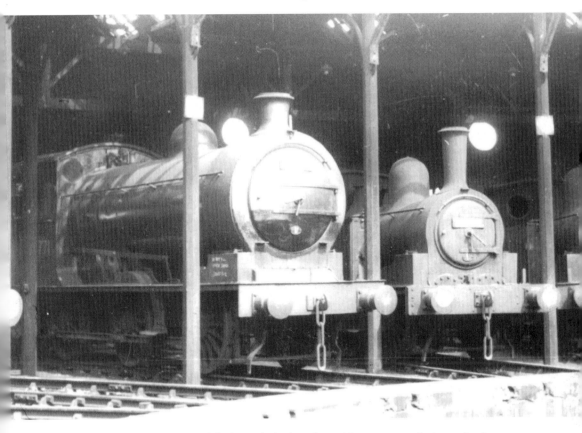

Sitting around the turntable at Middlesbrough shed are locos Nos 65771 and 68312. At closure in 1958, the allocation was as follows:

A5 4-6-2T	69830, 69831, 69834, 69842.
A8 4-6-2T	69860, 69866, 69869, 69882, 69891.
J25 0-6-0	65270.
J26 0-6-0	65737, 65775, 65776, 65779.
J27 0-6-0	65870.
J50 0-6-0T	68908, 68942, 68948.
J71 0-6-0T	68245, 68260, 68292, 68312.
J72 0-6-0T	68684, 68688, 68689, 68690, 68712, 68721, 68740, 69006, 69019.
L1 2-6-4T	67754, 67759, 67764, 67765, 67766.
Q6 0-8-0	63340, 63349, 63355, 63364, 63368, 63369, 63373, 63375, 63380, 63393, 63396, 63401, 63405, 63409, 63411, 63417, 63420, 63424, 63435, 63442, 63452.
LMR 4MT 2-6-0	43054, 43057, 43071, 43072, 43073, 43102.

Total: 63. (H. Casserley)

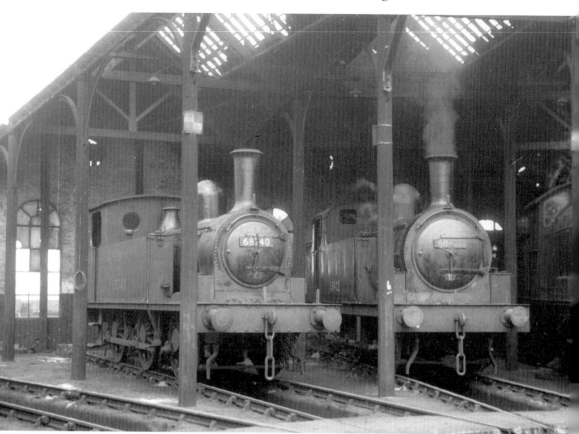

The end of the roundhouse at Middlesbrough in 1952, with ex-NER/LNER Worsdell Class J72 0-6-0T No. 68740 and another 0-6-0T, No. 68422 of Class J77. These engines were originally Fletcher 0-4-4 well tanks, built for the NER, but were rebuilt at York and Darlington as 4-foot-1-inch 0-6-0Ts between 1907 and 1921. The main function of Middlesbrough shed was to supply engines to works sidings at numerous iron and steel works on the south bank of the River Tees, together with shunting engines for the docks. Loads from the ironworks were worked to marshalling yards at Newport, west of Middlesbrough; the usual engines for these duties were 0-6-0 tender engines in 1923, so some twenty-eight such engines were allocated to the shed. Passenger turns out of Middlesbrough shed were mainly local, although in 1923 there were five return trips to Newcastle worked by Middlesbrough-allocated G5 0-4-4Ts. Over time, these trains became heavier and, in September 1938, when LNER corridor stock took over from NER vehicles, various classes were then tried on these Newcastle expresses, including A5 and A8 4-6-2Ts, D20 4-4-0s and J39 0-6-0s, but it was not until five V1 2-6-2Ts were received from Blaydon that these services were mastered. The five V1s, Nos 419, 423, 465, 479 and 484, arrived at Middlesbrough in January 1939. Until 1933, services to Whitby and Scarborough were worked by Saltburn shed, but with a change of route, Middlesbrough became more responsible for such trains. The A6 loco designed for the route in 1907 proved ineffective, and the most suitable engine found for working the heavy summer traffic was the J39 0-6-0. However, a derailment at Whitby put a stop to the use of these engines, and Class A8 4-6-2Ts were drafted on to the route as quickly as they could be rebuilt from the 4-4-4T locos originally used on the hilly line between Whitby and Scarborough, at Darlington works. Thus, when five A8s went to Blaydon in exchange for the V1s, some A8s were retained for Whitby and Scarborough services. Ten years later, V1 and V3 engines appeared on Scarborough workings after restrictions on their use south of Loftus were lifted. Back in 1923, local tank engine workings were to West

Hartlepool, Eston, Battersby, Eaglescliffe, Ferryhill, Port Clarence, Leamside, Saltburn and Darlington, although Middlesbrough had little involvement in Darlington–Saltburn workings. In winter, Scarborough services were worked by Sentinel steam railcar No. 2281 *Old John Bull* or Armstrong-Whitworth diesel-electric railcar *Tyneside Venturer*. The Sentinel usually worked Middlesbrough–Guisborough or Middlesbrough–Saltburn services. Around a year after the shed came under BR control, its allocation was as follows:

LNER code – M'BRO and BR code – 51D.

Q6 0-8-0	63256, 63260, 63272, 63281, 63282, 63283, 63289, 63328, 63333.
Q6 0-8-0	63351, 63364, 63368, 63375, 63409, 63411, 63417, 63420, 63442.
J39 0-6-0	64710, 64756, 64819, 64821, 64847.
J24 0-6-0	65687, 65710, 65726.
J26 0-6-0	65733, 65764, 65771, 65775, 65776, 65779.
G5 0-4-4T	67281, 67338.
V1 2-6-2T	67638, 67639, 67673.
V3 2-6-2T	67684, 67685, 67686, 67691.
J71 0-6-0T	68260, 68303, 68307, 68312.
J77 0-6-0T	68409, 68414, 68422, 68425.
J72 0-6-0T	68688, 68689, 68690, 68712, 68713, 68721, 68740, 68754, 69006, 69019.
A8 4-6-2T	69584, 69859, 69866, 69873, 69878.

Total: 64. (H. Casserley)

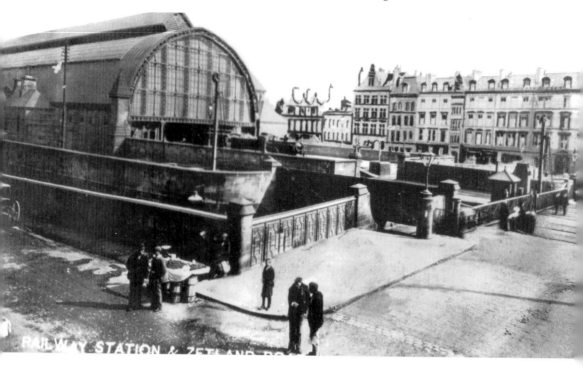

A more general view of Middlesbrough station at the end of the nineteenth century, with an NER loco in view. In 1829, a group of businessmen bought 527 acres of 'swampland' and established the 'Middlesbrough Estate Company', which planned to develop a new port and a suitable town to supply its labour. However, the new line only went as far as Newport in 1830, and it became very successful, so much so that Newport could not cope with the demands placed upon it. Thus, in 1839, work began on Middlesbrough Dock. This new dock was laid out by Sir William Cubitt, and the whole infrastructure was built by resident Civil Engineer George Turnbull. At a cost of £122,000 and after three years, the formal opening of the dock complex occurred on 12 May 1842; it was purchased by the S&DR on completion. (LOSA)

THE CLARENCE RAILWAY

In 1823, the Stockton group, who favoured a canal and, later, a railway, which would have run from Stockton to a point west of Darlington, promoted the Tees & Weardale Railway. Bills were submitted in 1824 and 1825, but both were rejected. Further changes were made, which meant that the proposed line would not reach Weardale, and its title was changed to 'The Clarence Railway' in honour of the Duke of Clarence, later William IV. The line was designed to challenge the monopoly of the S&DR; this ensured that it would run into trouble, as the S&DR placed difficulties in its way whenever possible. Despite these problems, the Clarence Railway was authorised on 23 May 1828. Its main line was to run from Haverton Hill and join the S&DR at Sim Pasture Farm, together with three branches which were 'to open a shorter course than heretofore between several valuable Mines of coal and the River Tees'.

The Clarence Railway had its first coal shipped from Stockton and, from January 1834, from Haverton Hill. In the same year, the line was extended to Port Clarence, and coal commenced being shipped from there using a single loading point.

Unfortunately, the Clarence Railway never reached the coalfields, and any coal consigned to it had to pass over S&DR metals for the first part of the journey. The S&DR levied a charge of 2.25d per ton a mile, which enabled the Darlington company to impose a 2s 6d charge on each Newcastle cauldron wagon of 53 hundredweight sent via the Clarence Railway, making transport costs more expensive, despite the distance being 5 miles shorter.

As a consequence, the Clarence Railway was never financially stable, and the situation was made worse by removal of the head office to London, with a new board of directors, at the request of the Exchequer Loan Commissioners. By 1842, the Clarence Railway owed some £149,394 to the Commissioners, who took charge of the line when the company could not meet its commitments and instructed that it should be sold. Some shareholders managed to raise £80,000, which staved off bankruptcy and allowed the railway to continue. The Clarence Railway was bought by the Hartlepool West Harbour & Dock Company on 30 June 1852.

Shortly before the First World War, part of the Clarence Railway was electrified so that coal from the collieries in West Durham could be moved to marshalling yards at Newport faster and more economically. The section so treated was from Simpasture Junction to Carlton (Redmarshall), and thence via the west to south curve to join the Wellfield–Bowesfield line of 1877, running along the S&DR Middlesbrough extension of 1830. Electrification was completed on 1 July 1915, but wartime restrictions on shipment of coal gave the line a difficult start. After the war, traffic did not increase significantly, and by 1934, when extensive renewals of overhead equipment were becoming due, electric traction was abandoned in favour of steam. On 7 January 1935, the marshalling yards at Shildon were closed, the loco shed closing in the following July. The ten electric locomotives were sent to Darlington for storage and, with one exception, never ran again, but were not broken up until 1950.

Traffic over this route continued until 1963, when the section between Simpasture Junction and Stillington North Junction was closed.

Opposite: A map of the Clarence Railway, showing its connections to the Stockton & Hartlepool Railway and the West Hartlepool Dock & Railway Company. The Clarence Railway also made head-on connections with the Stockton & Darlington Railway at Stockton and West Auckland. (Author)

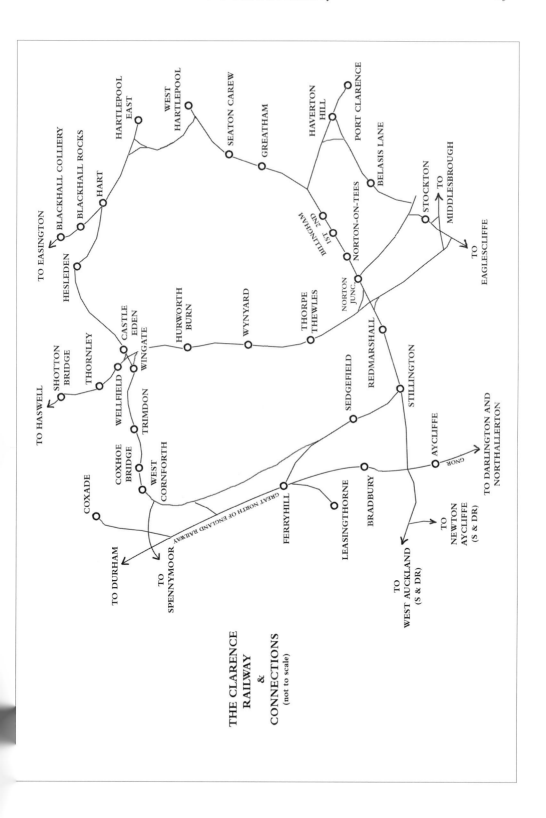

THE CLARENCE RAILWAY & CONNECTIONS (not to scale)

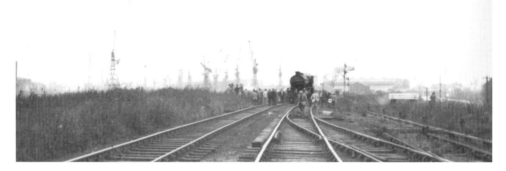

Port Clarence as it appeared on 28 September 1963, looking from the dead end. Ex-LNER Class B1 No. 61037 *Jairou* is seen in the distance, having become derailed after running round a special train. The first coals shipped from the Clarence Railway went from Stockton, and, from January 1834, from Haverton Hill. In the same year, the Clarence Railway was extended to Port Clarence, and coal was loaded using a single loading point. As traffic increased, it was proposed, on 7 April 1881, that a new shed for nine locomotives be provided at Port Clarence, and it was recommended that a portion of a shed then standing at Clarence Junction, Stockton, should be removed and re-erected at Port Clarence to form the shed, at a cost of £300. By 1898, seven engines were based at Port Clarence for use on freight and mineral traffic on the north bank of the Tees. The last record of a shed at Port Clarence was in January 1915, when Class 398 0-6-0 No. 886 was withdrawn from the shed.

A new four-road double-ended shed at Haverton Hill was authorised in November 1896, and a tender of £5,849 3s 1d was accepted in June 1897. Primarily a freight shed, it did provide a loco, a Class F8 2-4-2T, to work a passenger service between Billingham and Port Clarence. However, by 1939, the shed had lost all of its passenger turns.

Haverton Hill shed allocation in 1949 was as follows:

BR code: 51G.
Q5 0-8-0   63311, 63314.
Q6 0-8-0   63340, 63367, 63374, 63405, 63407, 63416, 63423, 63425, 63443, 63446,
                63453.
J25 0-6-0   65660.
J27 0-6-0   65787, 65805, 65830, 65853, 65855, 65859, 65865.
Total: 21.

The shed finally closed on 13 June 1959, and the majority of its allocation was transferred to the new shed at Thornaby. Locomotives transferred to Thornaby at closure were:

B1 4-6-0   61018 *Gnu.*
B1 4-6-0   61021 *Reitbok.*
B1 4-6-0   61024 *Addax.*
B1 4-6-0   61037 *Jairou.*
B1 4-6-0   61255.
Q6 0-8-0   63341, 63343, 63344, 63347, 63361, 63367, 63374, 63382, 63407, 63416,
                63432, 63443, 63446.
WD 2-8-0   90086, 90397, 90479.
Total: 21. (H. Casserley)

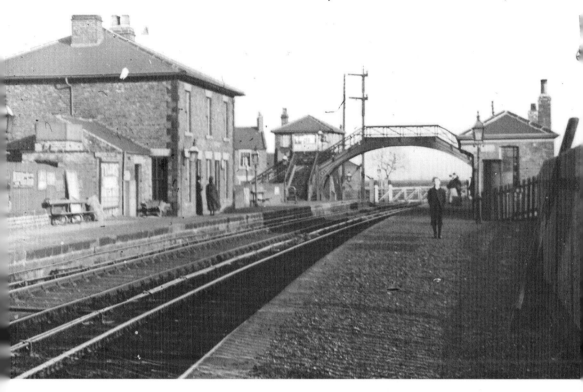

From Haverton Hill, the Clarence Railway headed south to Stockton, via Belasis Lane, where it met the S&DR and the Leeds Northern Railway. Also, going west from the junction with the line to Hartlepool, the railway entered Billingham, now famous for steel manufacture; its station is seen here early in the twentieth century. From here, the line passed through Norton-on-Tees before reaching Norton Junction. (LOSA)

PORT CLARENCE and BILLINGHAM (Auto-cars).—North Eastern.

Up.						Week Days.											Sundays.			
	mrn	mrn	mrn	mrn	mrn	aft	aft	aft	aft	aft	aft	aft	aft	aft	aft	mrn	mrn	aft	aft	aft
ort Clarence....dep.	5 55	7 0	8 0	9 20	1036	1210	12s30	1 5	2 30	4 20	5 5	5 32	6 18	7 8	8s15	5 53	9 55	8 10	9 12	5 50	7 0	8 57
averton Hill....[710	6 2	7 4	8 4	9 24	1040	1214	12s34	1 9	2 34	4 24	5 9	5 36	6 22	7 12	8s20	8 57	9 59	8 14	9 16	5 54	7 4	9 1
llingham 708, arr.	6 7	7 8	8 8	9 28	1044	1218	.....	1 13	2 38	4 28	5 13	5 40	6 26	7 16	....	9 1	....	8 18	9 20	5 58	7 8	9 5
08 W. Hartlepool ar.	.....	7 42	8 35	9 53	1110	1245	.....	....	3 4	4 59	....	6 5	6 46	7 53	....	9 49	....	....	9 46	....	7 32	9 32

Down.							Week Days.									Sundays.			
	mrn	mrn	mrn	mrn	mrn	mrn	aft	aft	aft	aft	aft	aft	aft	aft	aft	aft	mrn	mrn	aft	aft	aft	aft
10 W. Hartlepool dp	....	5 34	6 57	8 50	10 0	1122	1211	1 13	2 55	4 24	4 43	5 40	....	7 5	....	8 54	8 10	....	....	5 48	7 50	....
llingham ....dep.	....	6 9	7 25	9 10	1022	1143	1235	1 35	3 19	4 48	5 18	6 5	6 40	7 38	....	9 34	8 34	9 35	....	6 13	8 12	9 15
averton Hill........	5 45	6 14	7 29	9 14	1026	1147	1239	1 39	3 23	4 52	5 22	6 9	6 44	7 42	8s25	9 38	8 38	9 39	5 40	6 17	8 16	9 19
ort Clarence....arr.	5 49	6 19	7 33	9 18	1030	1151	1243	1 43	3 27	4 56	5 26	6 13	6 48	7 46	8s29	9 42	8 42	9 43	5 44	6 21	8 20	9 23

s Saturdays only.

A 1910 timetable for autocar services between Port Clarence and Billingham. (Author's collection)

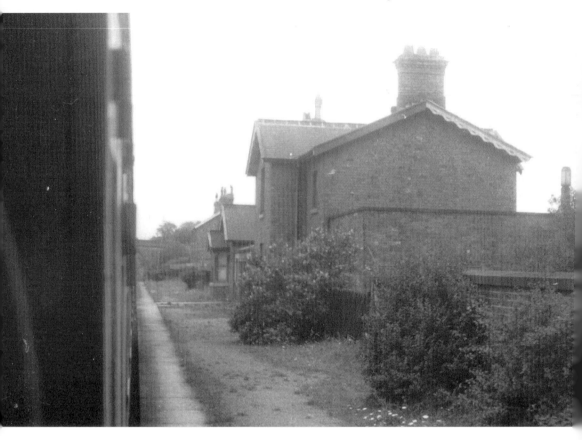

Running north from Norton Junction, the first station was at Thorpe Thewles, seen here on 2 September 1956. (R. Casserley)

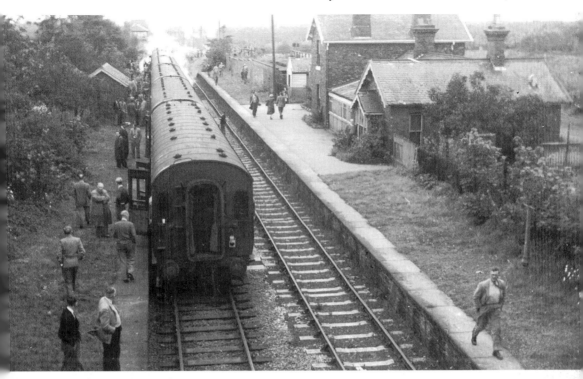

The next station north was at Wynyard, seen here looking towards Stockton, with a special train visiting, in September 1956. (R. Casserley)

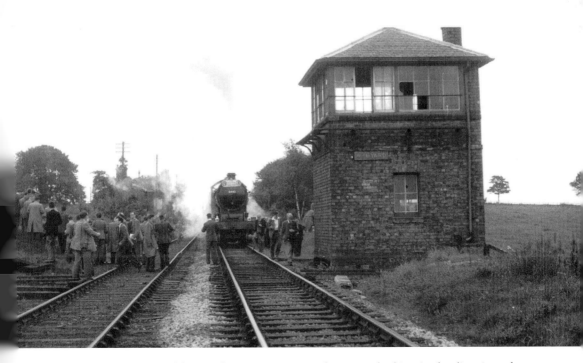

On the same day, the signal box and station at Wynyard are seen looking in the direction of Sunderland. (H. Casserley)

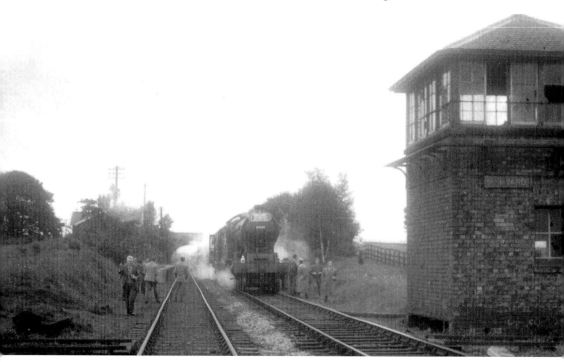

Above: Waiting at Wynyard station at the head of a special train on 2 September 1956 is ex-LNER Class B16 4-6-0 No. 61443. (R. Casserley)

Opposite bottom: Running further north and passing the junction for West Cornforth, Ferryhill and Hart, where it joins the line from Hartlepool East to Easington, lay the station at Wellfield, seen here facing Stockton in September 1956, with B16 No. 61443 having recently arrived with its special train. At Ferryhill, a loco shed, which was estimated to cost £2,780, was authorised in 1879 to hold nine engines. Although it was yet another goods shed, it did have one passenger turn at 'Grouping', operated by a G5 0-4-4T, running to Battersby and Newcastle. By 1938, passenger workings were reduced to two on Saturdays, the first to Stockton, Middlesbrough and Battersby, while the second went to Battersby, returned as far as Stockton, then worked to Guisborough, then from Guisborough to Middlesbrough, thence by light engine to Stockton, then from Stockton to Ferryhill. On summer Sundays, one engine worked to Redcar and back, while the other worked to Seaton Carew and back if required. The shed was closed in 1938 and its allocation at this time was:

G5 0-4-4T	1882.
J21 0-6-0	800.
J25 0-6-0	1962, 1972, 1985, 1988, 1995, 2059, 2130, 2139.
J27 0-6-0	888, 1064, 1066, 1222, 1229.
J39 0-6-0	1490.
J72 0-6-0T	581, 2326.
J73 0-6-0T	544, 545.
N9 0-6-2T	1651.
Q5 0-8-0	83, 430, 443, 474, 648, 773, 1186, 1685, 1696.
Total: 30.	

In 1939, some locos and rolling stock were evacuated from the railway museum at York to Ferryhill, returning to York in 1947 and in 1951. The building held surplus G5 0-4-4Ts, which included Nos 67242, 67272, 67294, 67318 and 67331. (R. Casserley)

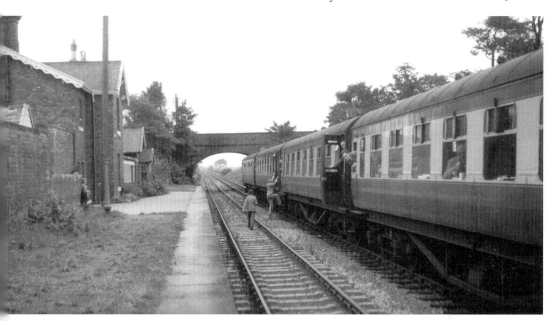

Another view of Wynyard station, looking north, as the special train is ready to depart. (H. Casserley)

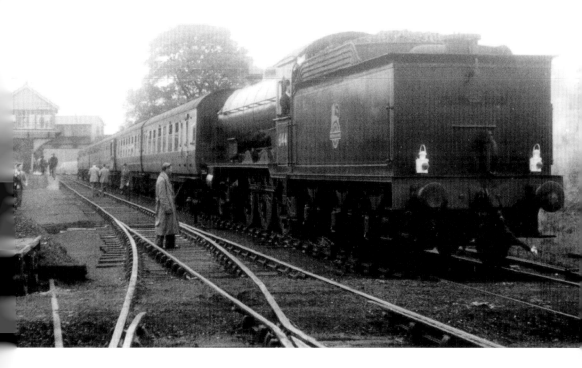

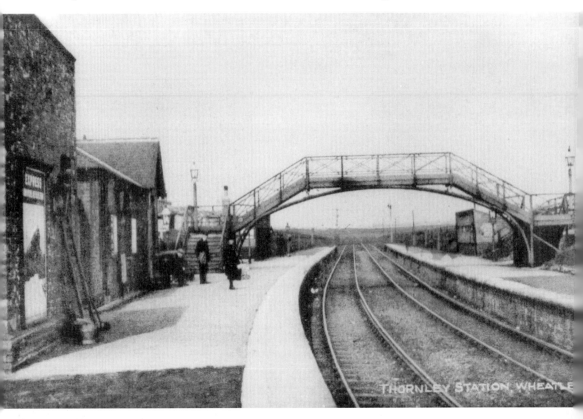

North from Wellfield was Thornley station, seen here in North Eastern Railway days. (LOSA)

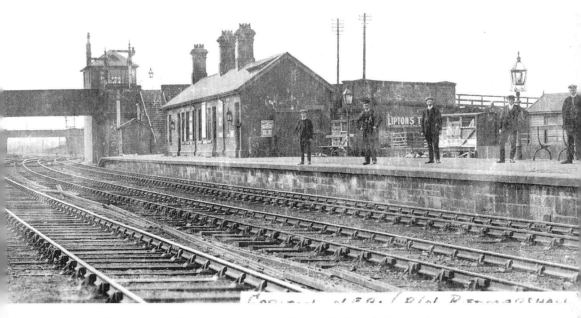

Running west from Norton Junction was the station at Redmarshall, seen here late in the nineteenth century. The line here ran to Stillington, where it joined the S&DR for access to West Auckland, and was useful to the Clarence Railway as it connected Port Clarence with the West Auckland coalfield. (LOSA)

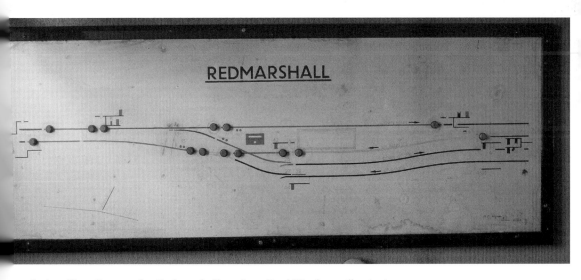

A signalling diagram for Redmarshall station. (Paul Hughes collection)

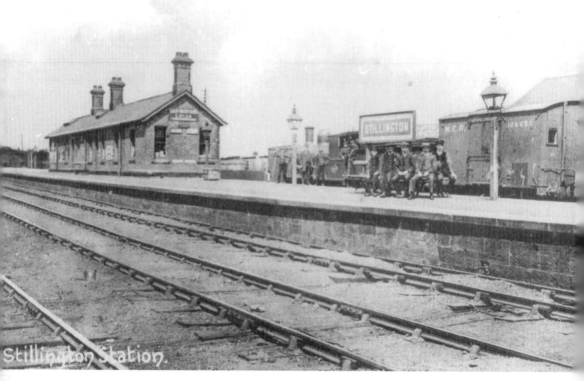

Running south-west from Redmarshall was Stillington station, which lay at the junction with the line to Ferryhill and West Cornforth. In 1829, the City of Durham branch and the Stockton branch were authorised, the former leaving the main line at Stillington Moor House and terminating at Old Elvet Street in Durham itself. Two more branches were also authorised: the Sherburn branch and the Byers Green branch, both of which left the City of Durham branch at Ferryhill. In 1832, the City of Durham branch was abandoned north of Shincliffe, and was not built north of Ferryhill, and the Sherburn branch only went as far as Coxhoe. Thus, only two branches were actually completed: to Stockton and Byers Green. The City of Durham branch reached Ferryhill on 16 January 1834 and, in 1835, the Sherburn branch was opened as far as Coxhoe. The Byers Green branch was opened on 31 March 1837 for mineral traffic, and passenger services between Stockton and Coxhoe commenced in January 1836, using horse-drawn coaches. Back on 2 February 1849, the station was witness to a boiler explosion, which caused two fatalities. (LOSA)

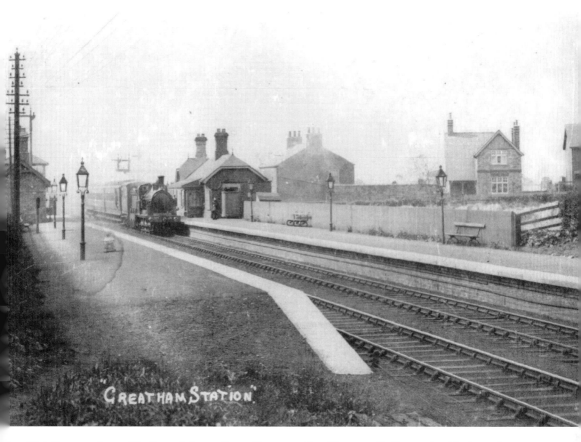

Heading north to Hartlepool from Port Clarence, the Clarence Railway passed through Greatham and Seaton Carew. A train, headed by an unidentified NER 0-6-0, is seen arriving at Greatham station early in the twentieth century. (LOSA)

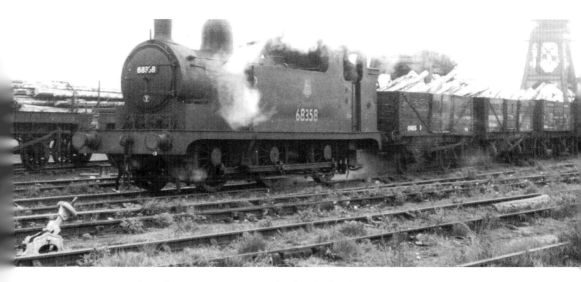

Arriving at West Hartlepool on 17 May 1952 with a load of timber is ex-NER/LNER Worsdell Class J73 0-6-0, No. 68358, with a dockside crane beyond. (H. Casserley)

NEWCASTLE, WEST HARTLEPOOL, STOCKTON, and MIDDLESBROUGH.—North Easter[n]

Miles from W. H'pool.	Up.		Week Days. Except Mondays. mrn	mrn	mrn	mrn	mrn	mrn	mrn	mrn	mrn	mrn	mrn	mrn	mrn	mrn	mrn	aft	aft	aft	aft	af
	754 Newcastle (Cen.)	dep.		....	4 55	5 5	6 25	....	7 5	8 17	....	....	9 17	10 0	....	....	11 17	....	....	....	1 17	....
	Hartlepool	dep.		5 19	....	6 23	7 20	7 59	....	9 0	9 15	....	10 0	1030	10 49	1145	....	....	1245	....	1 45	2
	West Hartlepool	"		5 28	....	6 55	7 48	8 8	....	9 16	9 25	....	1016	1055	11 18	12 5	12 15	....	1256	....	2 14	2
2¼	Seaton Carew			....	....	7 1	....	8 13	....	....	9 30	....	....	....	11 24	....	....	....	1 2	....	....	2
4½	Greatham			5 36	....	7 6	....	8 18	....	9 24	9 35	....	....	....	11 29	....	....	....	1 7	....	....	2
8	Billingham 767			5 43	....	7 13	....	8 24	....	....	9 41	....	....	....	11 37	....	....	....	1 16	....	....	2
9	Norton-on-Tees			....	....	7 16	....	....	....	....	....	....	....	....	11 40	....	....	....	1 19	....	....	2
11½	Stockton 740, 746, 753	arr.		5 54	....	7 25	7 58	8 36	....	9 37	9 53	....	1034	1113	11 49	1223	12 33	....	1 28	....	2 32	2
		dep.	5 30	....	7 10	7c35	8 37	....	9 10	9 40	....	1019	1038	1125	11c53	....	12 36	1 12	....	1 35	2 35	3 c
13¾	Thornaby		5 37	....	7 16	7c53	....	....	9 16	9 46	....	1025	....	1131	12c22	....	....	1 19	....	1 43	2 41	3c
15¾	Newport [756, 764		....	....	....	....	....	....	....	....	....	....	....	....	....	....	....	....	....	....	....	....
17	Middlesbrough 754,	arr.	5 45	....	7 22	7c59	8 47	....	9 22	9 52	....	1033	1049	1137	12c28	....	12 47	1 25	....	1 49	2 47	3c

Up.		Week Days—*Continued.* aft	aft	aft	aft	aft	aft	aft	aft	aft	aft	Sundays. mrn	mrn		Thro' Train to Darlington, see pages 753 and 757.	mrn	Arrives Port Clarence at 8 46 aft., see page 764.	a
754 Newcastle (Central)	dep.	....	3 17	....	4 17	....	5 17	....	7 17	....	....	....	....	....		7 53		5
Hartlepool	dep	3 15	3 45	4 15	4 45	5 15	5 45	6 30	7 45	8 45	9 45	....	8 0	....		5 18		8
West Hartlepool	"	3 25	4 14	4 38	5 15	5 37	6 16	6 50	8 15	8 55	10 15	....	8 10	....		5 43		8
Seaton Carew		3 31	....	4 43	....	5 43	....	6 55	....	9 0	10 21	....	8 15	....		5 48		8
Greatham		3 36	....	4 48	....	5 48	....	7 0	....	9 5	10 26	....	8 20	....		5 53		8
Billingham 767		3 44	....	4 55	....	5 56	....	7 7	....	9 11	10 33	....	8 28	....		6 1		8
Norton-on-Tees		3 47	....	4 58	....	5 59	....	7 10	....	....	....	....	8 31	....		6 4		
Stockton 740, 746, 753	arr.	3 56	4 32	5 8	5 33	6 8	6 34	7 19	8 33	9 24	10 46	....	8 40	....		6 13		
	dep.	4 10	4 35	5c14	5 40	....	6 37	7 43	8 36	9c26	10c49	5 30	8c44	....		6c16		
Thornaby		4 17	4 41	5c28	5 46	....	6 43	7 49	8 42	10c48	11c20	5 36	9c21	....		8c51		
Newport [764		....	....	....	....	....	....	....	....	....	....	....	....	....		....		
Middlesbrough 754, 756,	arr.	4 23	4 47	5c34	5 52	....	6 49	7 55	8 48	10c54	11c26	5 49	9c27	....		9c 2		

Miles.	Down.		Week Days. Except Mons. mrn	mrn	mrn	mrn	mrn	mrn	mrn	mrn	mrn	mrn	mrn	mrn	mrn	mrn	mrn	mrn	aft	aft	aft	a
	Middlesbrough	dep.	....	6 25	....	7 10	7 25	....	8 20	....	8 45	9 20	....	1020	....	10 55	1120	....	12 10	....	2 20	..
1¼	Newport		....	....	....	....	....	....	....	....	....	....	....	....	....	....	....	....	....	....	....	
3¼	Thornaby		....	6 31	....	7 16	....	....	....	....	8 51	9 26	....	1026	....	....	1126	....	12 16	....	....	
5½	Stockton 740, 753, 764	arr.	....	6 39	....	7 24	7 35	....	8 31	....	8 59	9 31	....	1031	....	11 6	1131	....	12 25	....	2 31	..
		dep.	5 17	6 45	7 10	....	7 37	8 10	8 33	8 45	9 1	9 33	9 49	1033	1041	....	1133	1145	12 40	1 4	2 33	2
8	Norton-on-Tees			....	7 17	....	....	8 17	....	8 52	....	....	....	....	1048	....	....	....	12 47	....	....	2
9	Billingham 767			....	7 22	....	....	8 21	....	8 56	....	....	....	....	1052	....	....	....	12 51	....	....	2
12¾	Greatham			....	7 29	....	....	8 28	....	9 3	....	....	....	....	1059	....	....	1158	12 58	....	....	2
14¾	Seaton Carew [754			....	7 34	....	....	8 33	....	9 8	....	....	....	....	11 4	....	....	12 3	1 3	....	....	3
17	West Hartlepool 740,	arr.	5 35	....	7 40	....	7 55	8 38	8 53	9 13	....	9 53	10 7	1053	11 9	....	1153	12 8	1 8	1 22	2 53	3
19½	Hartlepool	"	6 13	....	7 52	....	8 21	8 51	9 6	9 36	....	10 6	1021	11 6	1136	....	12 6	1221	....	1 36	3 6	3
49¾	754 Newcastle (Cen.)	arr.	6 42	8 58	....	9 16	9 35	....	9 52	....	1020	1052	1135	1154	....	....	1252	2 11	....	2 23	3 54	..

Down.		Week Days—*Continued.* aft	aft	aft	aft	aft	aft	aft	aft	aft	aft	aft	aft	aft	Sundays. mrn	mrn	Leaves Port Clarence at 6.30 aft., see page 764.	aft	Thro' Train from Darlington, see pages 756 & 752.	a
Middlesbrough	dep.	3 20	4 20	....	5 20	....	5 51	6 45	7 45	....	8c13	9c19	9c54	....	....	7c18		....		6
Newport		....	....	....	....	....	....	....	....	....	....	....	....	....	....	....		....		
Thornaby		....	....	....	....	....	5 57	6 53	7 53	....	8c20	9 c27	10 c 1	....	....	7c31		....		6
Stockton 740, 753, 764	arr.	3 31	4 31	....	5 31	....	6 7	6 59	8 1	....	9c35	10c20	10c41	....	....	9c21		....		8
	dep.	3 33	4 33	4 38	5 33	5 40	6 33	7 18	8 25	8 11	9 40	10 23	10 45	1123	5 17	9 25		....		9
Norton-on-Tees		....	....	4 45	....	5 47	....	7 25	....	....	....	....	....	....	....	9 32		....		9
Billingham 767		....	....	4 49	....	5 52	....	7 29	....	....	9 49	10 32	....	....	....	9 36		6 46		9
Greatham		....	....	4 56	....	5 59	....	7 36	....	....	9 56	b	....	....	....	9 43		6 53		9
Seaton Carew		....	....	5 1	....	6 4	....	7 41	....	8 27	....	....	....	....	....	9 48		6 58		9
West Hartlepool 740, 754	arr.	3 53	4 53	5 6	5 53	6 9	6 53	7 46	....	8 32	10 4	10 48	11 3	1141	5 35	9 53		7 3		9
Hartlepool	"	4 9	5 6	5 21	6 6	6 21	7 6	8 9	....	8 54	1036	....	11 16	1151	6 6	10 6		7 41		9
754 Newcastle (Central)	arr.	4 52	5 54	....	6 52	....	7 57	1080	1013	1110	....	....	....	....	6 37	6 31		9 6		

b Stops when required to set down.
c Via Eaglescliffe.
s Saturdays only.

☞ **For Local Trains** BETWEEN Hartlepool & West Hartlepool . . PAGE below

* * * **For other Trai[ns]** BETWEEN Thornaby and Middlesbrough. . West Hartlepool & Middlesbrou[gh]

HARTLEPOOL and WEST HARTLEPOOL.—North Eastern.

Hartlepool to West Hartlepool at 5 19, 6 23, 7 5, 7 20, 7 59, 8 30, 8 45, 9, 9 15, 9 30, 9 45, 10, 10 15, 10 30, 10 49, and 11 45 mrn.; 12 15, 12 30, 12 45, 1 15, 1 45, 2 15, 2 30, 2 45, 3 15, 3 30, 3 45, 4 15, 4 30, 4 45, 5 15, 5 30, 5 45, 6 15, 6 30, 7, 7 15, 7 45, 8 15, 8 30, 8 45, 9, 9 15, 9 45, 10 15, 10 45, and 11 25 aft. SUNDAYS at 6 25, 7 5, 8, and 10 13 mrn., 4 25, 6 55, 7 46, 8, 8 25, and 10 aft.

West Hartlepool to Hartlepool at 6 7, 6 42, 7 46, 8 15, 8 35, 8 45, 9, 9 15, 9 30, 9 45, 10, 10 15, 10 30, 11, and 11 30 [m]rn.; 12 noon, 12 15, 12 30, 1, 1 30, 2, 2 15, 2 30, 3, 3 15, 3 30, 4 3, 4 15, 4 30, 5, 5 15, 5*e*27, 5 30, 6, 6 15, 6 30, 6 45, 7, 7 30, 8 3, 8 30, 8 48, 9, 9 30, 10, 10 30, 11 10, and 11 45 aft. SUNDAYS at 6, 10 and 10 20 mrn., 5 5, 7 35, 7 50, 8 15, 9 45, and 10 15 [aft].

e Except Saturdays. Time on journey, 6 minutes.

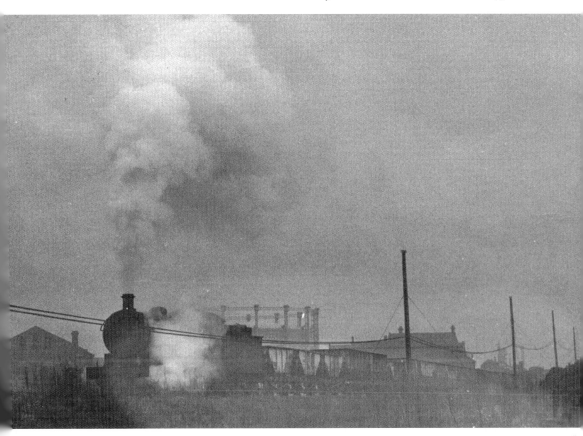

An evening view of West Hartlepool on 21 May 1966, very near the end of steam traction, showing an unidentified ex-LNER loco with a train of hopper wagons, probably heading for the docks. Industrial buildings and a gasometer provide the background scene. (Author's collection)

Opposite: A 1910 timetable for NER trains running between Newcastle and Middlesbrough, via Stockton and West Hartlepool. Also, below is the timetable for the shuttle service between West Hartlepool and (East) Hartlepool. (Author's collection)

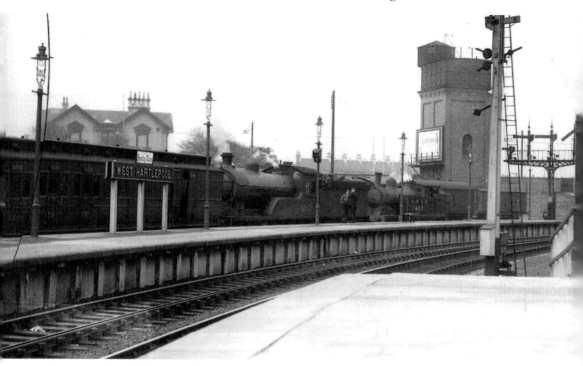

West Hartlepool station as it appeared on 13 May 1936, with a Class D20 4-4-0, No. 1217, in company with what appears to be a G5 0-4-4T, No. 437. In the background is the water tower, with the loco shed nearby. After the WHH&R was taken over by the NER in 1865, it was deemed that additional accommodation was required, and it was recommended that a new shed be built in August 1866. Approval for this was agreed in February 1867, but the project was cancelled. In December 1869, a report stated that an engine shed was definitely required at West Hartlepool and, six months later, a tender for £6,093 16s 9d was accepted, with the building being completed at the end of 1871. On 9 January 1874, the north end of the old West Hartlepool shed was blown down, and the south end had to be demolished. Two months later, the building of a new shed was planned and the blown-down shed was to be re-erected. A tender of £2,616 6s 8d was accepted for the rebuilt shed, and another tender of £9,993 accepted to build the new shed. No further work was then done at West Hartlepool shed.

Turns at West Hartlepool in 1922/3 were three to Harrogate, which were worked by 4-4-0 locos. Seven other duties were mainly operated between Newcastle, South Shields, Middlesbrough and Ferryhill; one even went as far as Whitby, while another went to Thirsk. Two minor turns worked to Stockton and Hartlepool. A BTP (G6) 0-4-4T, with a driving coach at each end, worked between West Hartlepool and Hartlepool from 8.35 a.m. to 11.31 p.m. each weekday. Local services were worked by G5 0-4-4Ts. (H. Casserley)

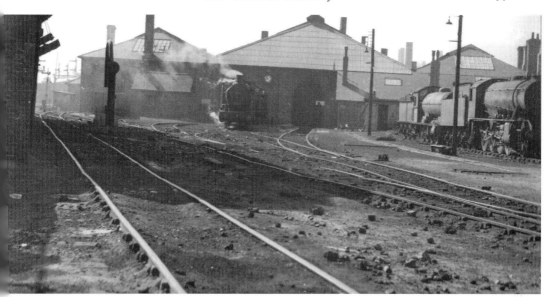

A general view of West Hartlepool loco shed on 30 August 1959, with an ex-WD 2-8-0 just in view on the right and a couple of ex-LNER classes.

The allocation for 1949 was as follows:

BR code: 51C.

D20 4-4-0	62372, 62379.
Q6 0-8-0	63355, 63373, 63383, 63392, 63396, 63397, 63401, 63410, 63414, 63415, 63419, 63421, 63422, 63424, 63427, 63435, 63438, 63452, 63454, 63457.
J39 0-6-0	64862, 64916, 64978.
J26 0-6-0	65747, 65748.
J27 0-6-0	65782, 65790, 65803, 65816, 65818, 65820, 65846, 65866.
G5 0-4-4T	67271, 67291, 67314, 67316, 67331, 67343.
J94 0-6-0ST	68042, 68053, 68054, 68055, 68056, 68057.
J71 0-6-0T	68233, 68244, 68248, 68258, 68263, 68276, 68290, 68291, 68295, 68301, 68302, 68306.
J73 0-6-0T	68355, 68358, 68359, 68364.
J72 0-6-0T	68683, 68684, 68685, 68692, 68694, 68697, 68703, 68711, 68716, 68734.
A8 4-6-2T	69862, 69863, 69864, 69871, 69893.
Total: 78.	

Under BR ownership, West Hartlepool was the first shed to receive diesel shunters for use in the extensive timber yards in the dock area, superseding some J71, J72 and J73 0-6-0Ts. (R. Carpenter)

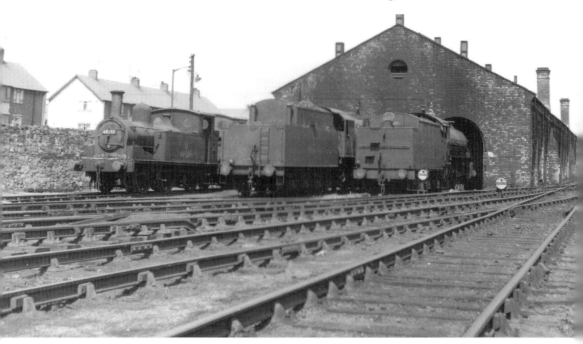

Another view of West Hartlepool loco shed on 3 July 1960, with an 0-6-0T in view and a pair of ex-WD engines seen to its right.

With closure on 17 September 1967, nine steam locos went for scrap and fourteen diesel shunters went to Thornaby.

The final allocation at West Hartlepool was:

Q6 0-8-0	63344, 63387.
WD 2-8-0	90074, 90076, 90360, 90478, 90627, 90677, 90695.
Diesel shunters	D2067, D2068, D2070, D2076, D2078, D2099, D2149, D2153, D2204, D2205, D2340, D3137, D3672.

Total:
Steam locos: 9.
Diesel locos: 13. (R Carpenter)

Opposite top: The Stockton & Hartlepool Railway connected West Hartlepool with the Clarence Railway, and was opened for goods on 12 November 1839 and to passengers on 1 December 1839. The station, named Hartlepool West, was opened on 9 February 1841, and was renamed West Hartlepool from February 1848. This station was closed on 3 May 1880, when replaced by a new station. West Hartlepool station was renamed Hartlepool on 26 April 1967 when West Hartlepool merged with (East) Hartlepool. Here, on 13 May 1936, LNER Class D20 4-4-0 No. 2027 is arriving at West Hartlepool with an express. (H. Casserley)

Opposite bottom: On the same day, LNER Class D20 4-4-0, No. 1252, prepares to depart from West Hartlepool with the 11.20 a.m. Middlesbrough–Newcastle service. In the background is the six-cylinder, 100 hp Sentinel steam railcar No. 2238 *Celerity*, working a local service to Sunderland. This railcar was first allocated to Hull Botanic Gardens from 7 April 1932, and worked local services between Hull and Bridlington. The railcar was then transferred to Sunderland from 6 July 1936, where it remained until withdrawal in February 1943. (H. Casserley)

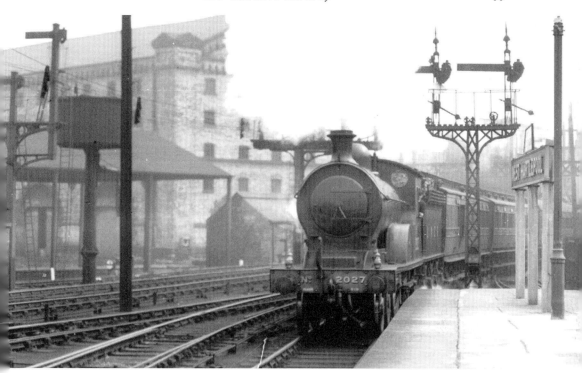

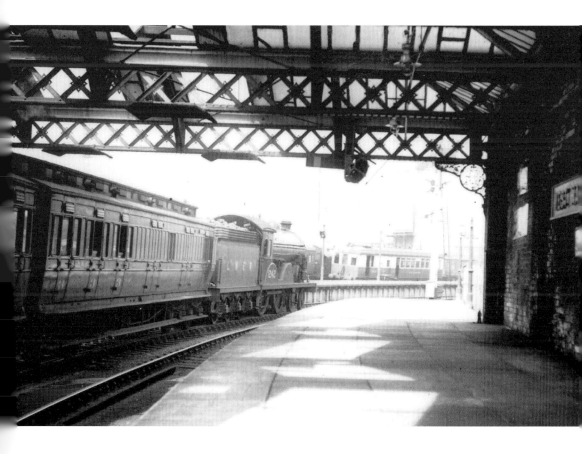

WEST HARTLEPOOL, SEAHAM, and SUNDERLAND.—North Eastern.

Miles	Up.					Week Days.															Sundays.				
		mrn	mrn	mrn	mrn	mrn	mrn	**m**	aft	aft	**c**	aft	**m**	**m**	aft	aft	**c**	aft	**m**	aft	aft	aft	mrn	mrn	aft	aft	aft
—	West Hartlepool ....dep.		6 45	8 17	8 44	....	1040	1140	....	1 2	2 3	3 20	....	4 28	....	5 36	6 12	....	8 18	....	1010	1027	....	5 38			
6¼	Horden		6 59	8 31	....	....	....	1154	....	2 20	....	....	4 42	....	....	6 29	....	8 32	....		1024	....					
—	Seaham..........dep. 5 10		....	....	....	1035	....	1253	....	3 44	....	5 20	....	....	8 20	....	....	....		1015	....		8 10	1 10	4 07	4 59	
12¾	Seaham Colliery 5 12	7 10	8 42	....	1037	....	12 5	1255	....	2 35	3 46	4 53	5 22	5 57	6 40	8 22	8 43	1017		1035	....		8 12	1 12	4 27	4 79	
15	Ryhope East 700... [701 5 18	7 16	8 48	....	1043	....	1211	1 1	....	2 37	3 52	4 59	5 28	....	6 46	8 28	8 49	1023		1041	....		8 18	1 18	4 87	5 39	
18	Sunderland 692, 699, arr. 5 24	7 22	8 54	9 13	1049	11 9	1218	7 1	30 2	43 3	49 3	55 5	36	6 52	8 34	8 55	1029		1047	1055	....		6	8 24	1 24	4 47	5 9	7 9

Miles	Down.					Week Days.															Sundays.				
		mrn	mrn	mrn	mrn	mrn	mrn	aft	aft	**e**	aft	aft	aft	aft	**m**	aft	aft	aft	aft	aft	aft	mrn	mrn	aft	aft	aft
—	New Station, Sunderland ....dep. 5 35	....	7 55	8 59	1 1010	1030	1043	12 7	1223	1 24	40 3	18 3	40 4	46 4	56	3 37	10 7	40 9	22 9	39 9	45	11 3 0	....	1115	7 45	1050	2 35	4 50	8
3	Ryhope East	5 42	....	8 12	....	1017	....	1055	1214	1230	....	1 47	3 25	3 47	....	5	3 6	10 7	17 7	47 9	29	9846 9 52	11 3 7	....	1122	....	1057	2 42	4 57	8
5½	Seaham Colliery	5 49	....	8 19	12	1023	....	11	1220	1236	....	1 53	3 32	3 53	4 56	5	10 6	16 7	23 7	54 9	35	9853 10	4 1	1813	1125	1129 7	56 11	4 2	49.5	4 78
5¾	Seaham ....arr. 5 51	....	....	....	1025	....	1222	1238	....	....	3 34	....	....	5 12	....	....	7 56	....	9855	....	....	....	1131	7 58	11 6	2 51.5	6 8
11½	Horden	6 15	....	8 29	....	....	1112	....	....	2 4	....	4 4	....	6 27	34	....	9e46	....	....	1013	....	....	1186				
18	West Hartlepool arr.	6 27	8 24	3 41	9 33	....	1057	1124	....	1 53	2 19	4 4	4 16	5 16	....	6 42	7 46	....	9e58	....	....	1013	....	1186				

e Stops at **Blackhall Rocks** (between West Hartlepool and Horden) on Wednesdays and Saturdays.
e Except Saturdays.   **g** Runs on the 2nd, 16th, and 30th instant.   **m** Auto-car.   **s** Saturdays only.
☞ For **OTHER TRAINS** between West Hartlepool and Sunderland, see page 700.

An NER timetable for trains between West Hartlepool and Sunderland. It was this service that was operated by Sentinel steam railcars under LNER auspices in the 1930s. (Author's collection)

SUNDERLAND, DURHAM (Elvet), STOCKTON, and WEST HARTLEPOOL.—North Eastern.

[Timetable: Up and Down services, Week Days and Sundays]

* Station for Easington (2½ miles).   † About 1 mile to Durham (Main) Station.   *a* Via Tyne Dock.
☞ For **OTHER TRAINS** between Newcastle, Sunderland, Stockton, and West Hartlepool, see page 754; between Sunderland and Durham, see page 742; between Castle Eden and West Hartlepool, see page 739.

A 1910 timetable for NER services between Sunderland and West Hartlepool, via Durham and Stockton. (Author's collection)

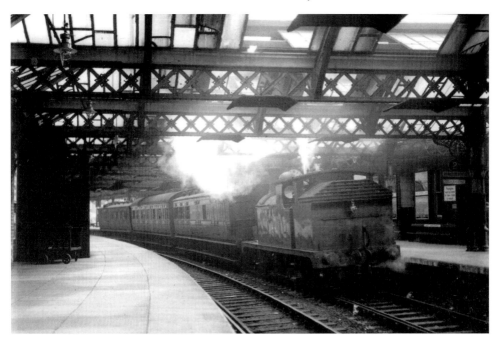

Just arrived at West Hartlepool with the 10.58 a.m. from Stockton, on 13 May 1936, is LNER Class G5 0-4-4T No. 437. (H. Casserley)

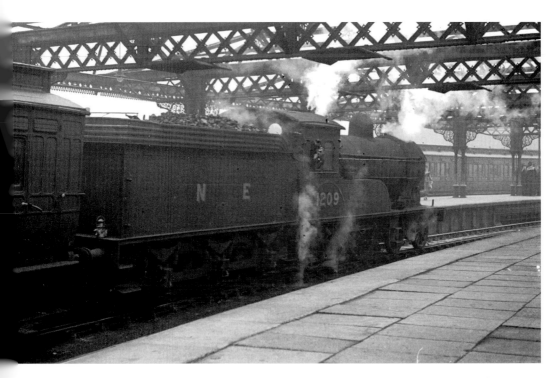

A decade later, on 20 October 1945, is LNER Class D20 4-4-0 No. 1209 waiting to depart from West Hartlepool. As can be seen, the loco is still sporting its wartime livery, the Second World War having only recently come to an end. (H. Casserley)

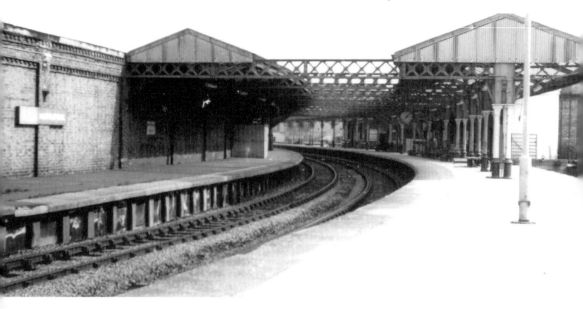

West Hartlepool station, facing Stockton, in BR days. (R. Casserley)

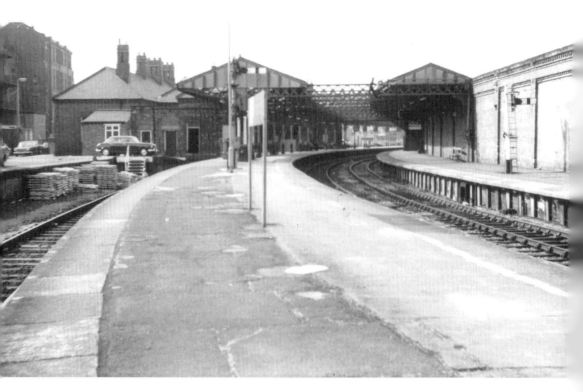

Another view of West Hartlepool station, facing Sunderland, in 1974, after the 'west' was dropped from the station name. (R. Casserley)

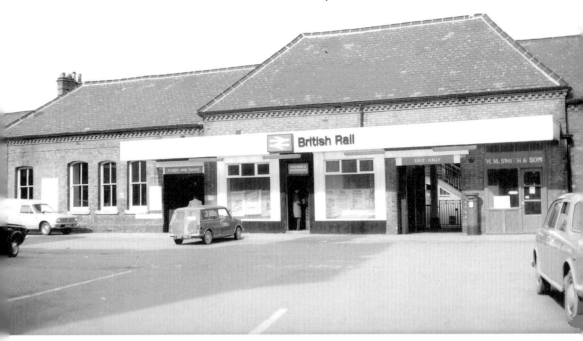

Exterior of (West) Hartlepool station as it appeared on 19 March 1974, with British-built cars in view, including a Mini Countryman and an Austin 1800. (R. Casserley)

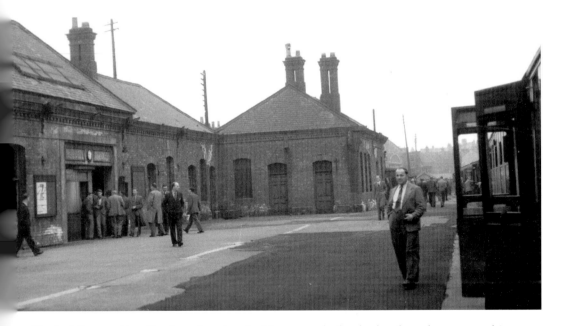

The buildings at East Hartlepool station, looking towards the dead end, as they appeared in 1956. (H. Casserley)

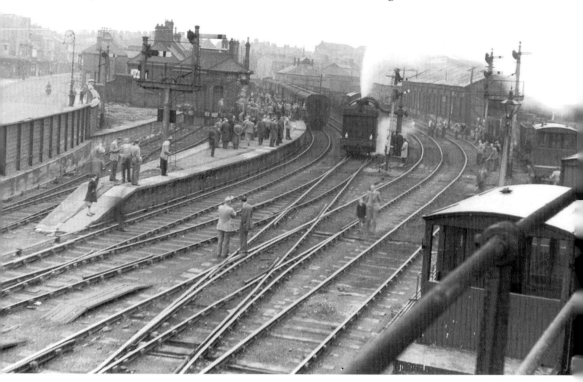

A general view of Hartlepool (East) station, facing the dead end, as it appeared on 2 September 1956, with a loco running round the special train it has just brought in. On the right are assorted brake vans outside the goods shed. Like West Hartlepool, an engine shed, which dated back to the early days of the railway and was made up of three separate buildings, was also situated here. An additional shed to house twelve engines was authorised in 1861, at a cost of £2,000, and was completed the following year. The shed at East Hartlepool housed freight and shunting engines and, in 1923, had only one passenger turn, from Hartlepool to Graythorpe Halt, on the Seaton Snook branch, for workmen. There were two passenger turns on Saturdays – one between West Hartlepool and Ferryhill and the other between Hartlepool, West Hartlepool, Sunderland and Newcastle – both worked by Class N8 0-6-2Ts, the shed having four in 1923. The shed was closed on 17 April 1939, and its all of its engines were transferred to West Hartlepool shed; all duties were worked from there.

East Hartlepool shed allocation at closure was as follows:

J24 0-6-0	1826.
J26 0-6-0	67, 1139, 1670, 1698.
J71 0-6-0T	77, 137, 176, 260, 541, 980, 1143, 1832.
J72 0-6-0T	1736, 1761, 1763, 2185, 2309, 2324, 2327.
J73 0-6-0T	547, 548, 552, 553.
J77 0-6-0T	953.
Q5 0-8-0	1215.
Q6 0-8-0	1284, 2230, 2239, 2262.
Total: 30.	

Both East Hartlepool and West Hartlepool were transferred to Middlesbrough District on 1 April 1933. (R. Casserley)

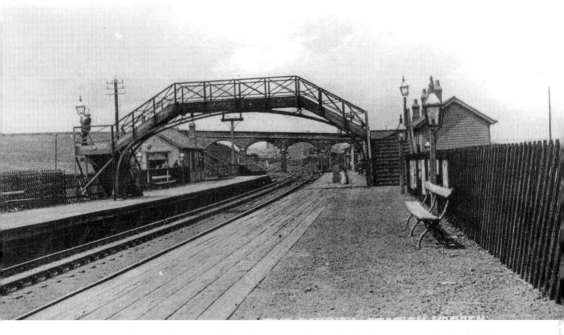

Heading north between Hartlepool and Washington, after Blackhall Rocks and Blackhall colliery, was the station at Horden, seen here in NER days. (LOSA)

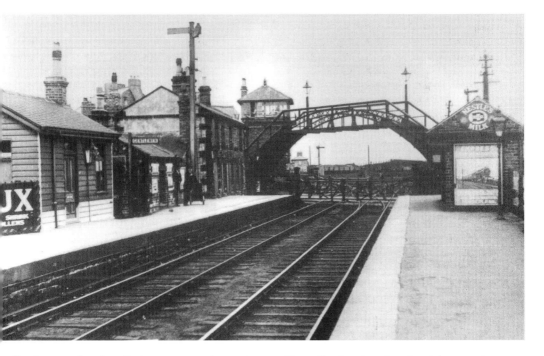

Further north, after Easington, was the station at Haswell, showing the signal box, main building and extensive sidings beyond the level crossing and footbridge. Note the enamel advertising signs, a common sight at railway stations in steam days, and so much part of the railway scene. (LOSA)

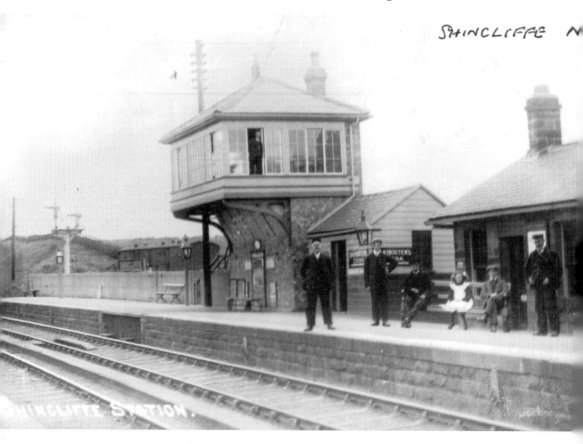

Shincliffe station in NER days, showing the signal box on the platform and the small station building, along with station staff and a family awaiting the arrival of a train. At one time, Shincliffe also had an engine shed, possibly from 1860, when rope haulage over the Durham & Sunderland Railway ceased. Use of locomotives on the branch before this time was restricted, and permission for their use had to be given in writing. An engine was based here to operate the Shincliffe–Sunderland (Hendon) service. It is believed that the shed ceased to exist around 1893. (LOSA)

Opposite top: Leamside station, showing the main building on the island platform, with a dead end in the centre. (LOSA)

Opposite bottom: Fencehouses station at the end of the nineteenth century, showing a typical NER footbridge and signal box beyond. Also in view outside the main buildings are the station staff, passengers and parcels awaiting collection. (LOSA)

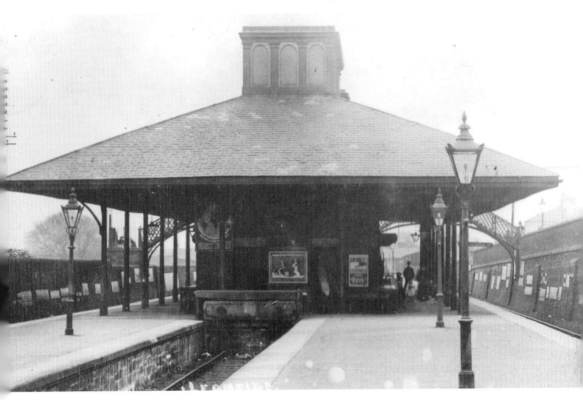

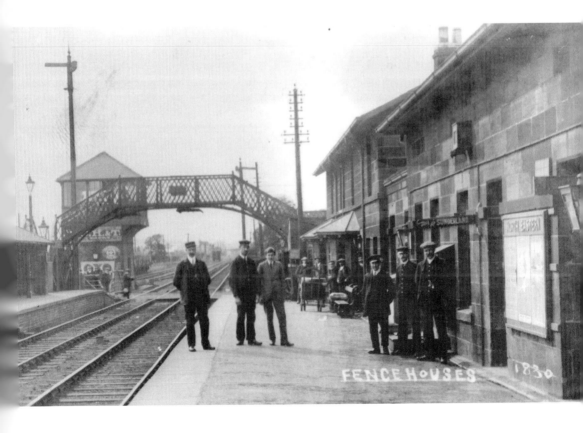

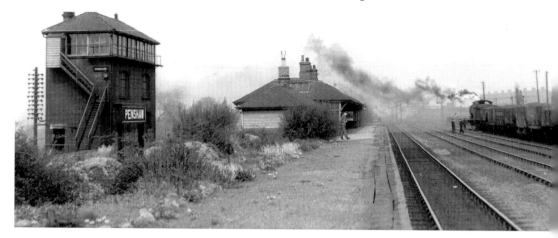

An atmospheric, but bleak, industrial landscape at Penshaw station on 30 April 1952, with the signal box and simple main building on the left. The signal box controls the sidings, from where an ex-LNER goods engine is labouring to leave with yet another loaded coal train after it has been coupled by staff standing at the side of the train. It was locations like this that made Britain, principally London and the South East, prosperous; those who worked hard for very little reward to bring the coal out of the ground were left to languish in a state of poverty when these pits became exhausted or uneconomic and were closed, leaving nothing to replace them. (H. Casserley)

LINES TO LOFTUS AND GUISBOROUGH

An early branch from Middlesbrough was the Middlesbrough & Redcar Railway, leased to the S&DR in 1847; both were taken over by the NER in 1863. Prior to NER control, the line was extended to Saltburn in 1861 as part of the Cleveland Railway, this line being extended to Loftus, where it would eventually join the Whitby, Redcar & Middlesbrough Railway for access to the seaside resort at Whitby. There was also a freight branch from Saltburn Junction to serve the Boulby Mine.

Extension of the line from Redcar to Saltburn meant that the original Redcar terminus was replaced on 19 August 1861. The extension opened up Redcar, Marske and Saltburn as seaside resorts, which served the population of Middlesbrough as well as areas further afield, the railways transporting these visitors.

The line between Middlesbrough and Saltburn remains open as part of the Tees Valley Line, and trains are operated by Northern Rail.

The Middlesbrough & Guisborough Railway was opened in 1853 and absorbed by the NER around a decade later. After takeover by the NER, a new station was built at Pinchinthorpe, and, in 1904, Hutton Gate station was purchased for public use. Pinchinthorpe station only lasted until shortly after the Second World War, closing in 1951. The remaining stations closed with the M&GR in 1964. A link was made with the Cleveland Railway in 1878 and was used for goods traffic until 1960. From Nunthorpe, the only section remaining open is that north to Middlesbrough, via Ormesby station, now serving as part of the Esk Valley line. Ormesby station was renamed Marton, keeping a Captain Cook connection, and a new station, Gypsy Lane, has also been opened.

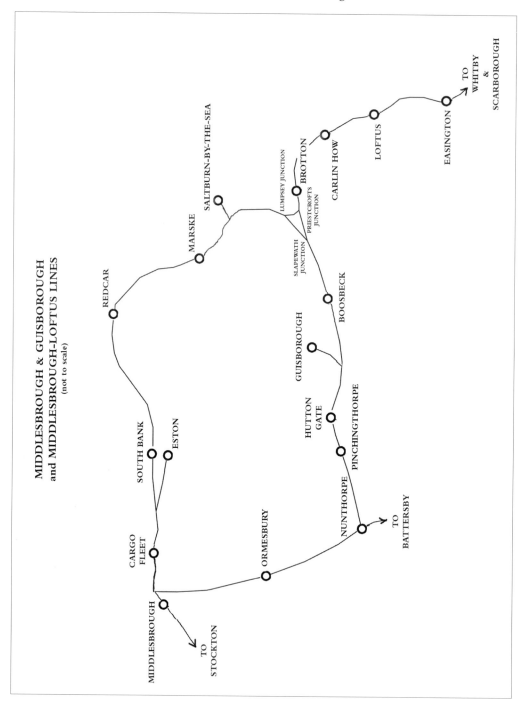

A map of the railway routes from Middlesbrough to Loftus, for Whitby and to Guisborough, along with the connection at Brotton for the Whitby and Saltburn lines. (Author)

...LINGTON, STOCKTON, MIDDLESBROUGH, REDCAR, and SALTBURN.—North Eastern.

SALTBURN, REDCAR, MIDDLESBROUGH, STOCKTON, and DARLINGTON.—North Eastern.

A NER timetable of 1910 for services along the line from Middlesbrough to Saltburn, with connections for Stockton and Darlington. (Author's collection)

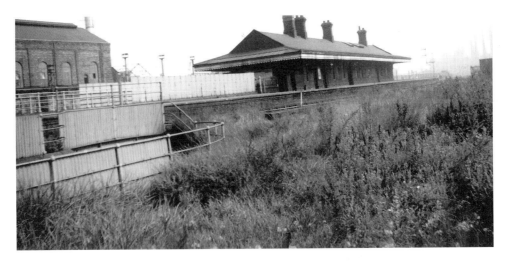

Cargo Fleet station, the first on the Middlesbrough–Saltburn line, as it appeared on 23 August 1970. The industrial nature of the area can be seen in this view, with chemical works in the background. The line on which the station stood was on flat land south of the River Tees, within a mile of the riverbank. A station was opened at Cargo Fleet in April 1947 and was originally named Cleveland Port. The name appeared in Bradshaw's Guide until 1867, Cargo Fleet being generally adopted after that. A new station was opened to serve Cargo Fleet, around 440 yards from the previous one, on 9 November 1885, and was built as an island within a multiple-track system, the line having expanded to cope with expanded freight and passenger traffic. Although Cargo Fleet was only a passenger station, several sidings were built nearby to serve two ironworks and a brickworks. This new station cost around £2,317 to build, and included material salvaged from Middlesbrough (Wood Street) station. Declining traffic, as many local industries closed in the 1980s, meant that the station saw little passenger traffic, and BR decided to close it despite objections from the local authority; only the island platform remained, until it was removed in 2002. (R. Casserley)

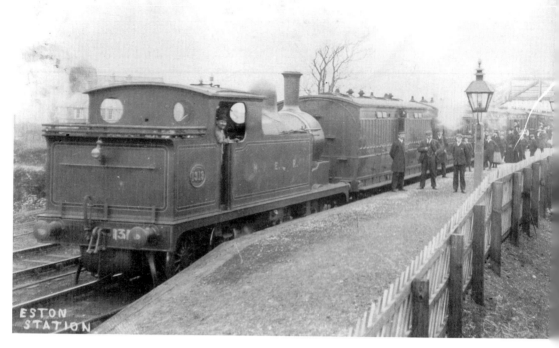

The terminus station at Eston, with an NER 0-4-4T (later LNER Class G5), No. 13119, about to depart with a local service to Middlesbrough. The station at Eston was opened by the NER on 1 January 1902 and continued to serve passengers until 1929, although the little branch remained open for goods traffic until 1966. The station was the terminus of a short spur of the Normanby Branch. This was the second station to bear the name Eston; the original, which was closed in November 1885, was replaced by South Bank station on a nearby site. In fact, the old Eston station was not in Eston itself, but 2 miles north at South Bank, an industrial area. The little branch left the main Middlesbrough–Saltburn line at Cargo Fleet and was accompanied by a couple of ironworks lines between Cargo Fleet and Eston, all of which were around 2 miles long. Eston station was close to the centre of the village and the recently developed mining community of California, and consisted of a single platform with a one-storey wooden building and coal depot behind. Although the station served a population of around 28,000 people, the station was not heavily used and only issued around 128 tickets a day in 1911. By 1925, under LNER auspices, there were only four passenger trains a day each way, with one extra on a Saturday, taking around fifteen minutes to cover the distance to Middlesbrough. The LNER closed the station on 11 March 1929 and replaced the train services with buses. Nothing now remains of the station, and modern housing now occupies the site. (LOSA)

	MIDDLESBROUGH and ESTON —North Eastern.															
Miles.	Down.	Week Days.						Miles.	Up.	Week Days.						
		mrn	mrn	aft	aft	aft	aft	W			mrn	mrn	aft	aft	aft	aft	aft
—	Middlesbrough..dep.	7 55	9 28	1 0	5 14	7 40	8 55	10 45	....	—	Eston ....dep.	8 15	9 48	18 20	2 10	5 35	8 0	9 52
1½	Cargo Fleet..........	7 59	9 32	1 4	5 18	7 44	8 59	....	....	3½	Cargo Fleet ......[above	8 26	9 59	18 31	2 21	5 45	8 11	9 53
4¼	Eston...........arr.	8 10	9 43	1 15	5 29	7 55	9 8	10 57	....	4¼	Middlesbrough, *see* arr.	8 29	10 2	18 34	2 24	5 48	8 14	9 5
		s Saturdays only.				W Wednesdays only.											

A 1910 NER timetable for infrequent passenger services between Middlesbrough and Eston, via Cargo Fleet. (Author's collection)

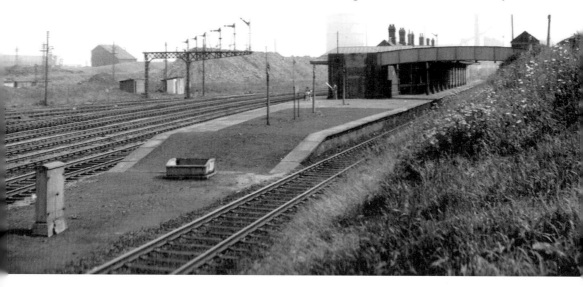

Looking towards Saltburn on the same day is South Bank station, a very similar structure to Cargo Fleet. By the 1980s, like Cargo Fleet, passenger numbers had fallen, and this South Bank station was closed; a new one was established 700 yards east to serve a new retail development in 1984. The local authority had hoped to keep Cargo Fleet open to serve the new Middlesbrough football stadium at Riverside, but the proposal failed. (R. Casserley)

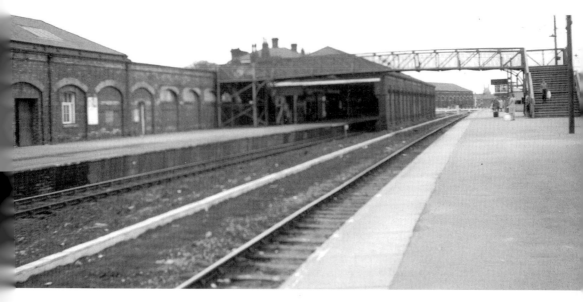

After leaving South Bank, the line passed through Grangetown station before climbing at a gradient of 1 in 242 to reach Redcar. The station at Redcar Central is seen here in August 1970. When the S&DR extended its line to Redcar in 1846, a loco shed here was authorised, and was built in August 1847 at a cost of £404 19s, but in September 1863 it was decided to move the shed to Saltburn. The original terminus at Redcar was replaced on 19 August 1861, when the line was extended to Saltburn. (R. Casserley)

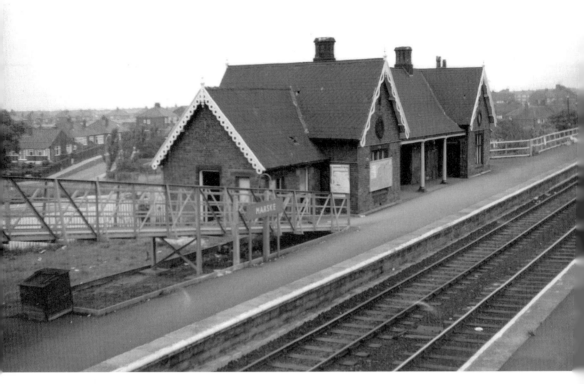

Marske station in 1970, built to serve the burgeoning holiday traffic in the town. (R. Casserley)

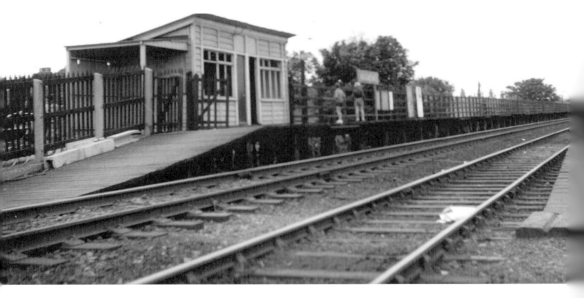

The simple halt at Redcar East, built in LNER days to serve local traffic. By this time, the town had been developed as a seaside resort and also had its own racecourse, which brought in extra traffic during race days, and extra capacity was needed to serve these passengers. By 1961, regular passenger services called at Redcar East. (R. Casserley)

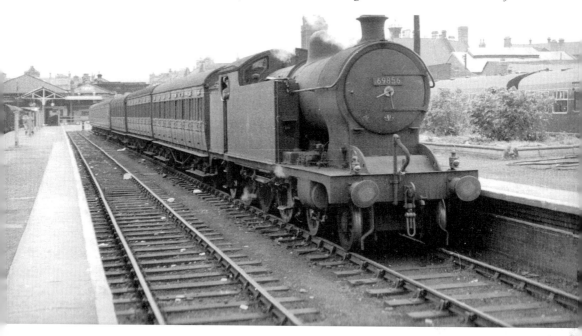

The terminus at Saltburn-by-the-Sea, to give the town its full title, was just known as 'Saltburn' station when it was photographed here, in September 1957, with ex-LNER A8 4-6-2T No. 69856 departing with a train for West Auckland. Replacement traction, in the form of a diesel multiple unit, can be seen on the far platform. (R. Carpenter)

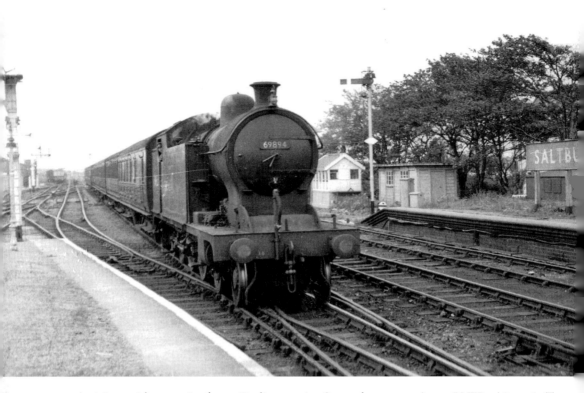

Arriving with a train from Darlington in September 1957 is ex-LNER A8 4-6-2T No. 69894. These locos were a common sight at Saltburn, as they were used to operate trains to Middlesbrough and Scarborough via Whitby (West Cliff) at this time. (R. Carpenter)

Opposite top: Standing at Saltburn station in September 1957 with its train is ex-LNER Class A8 4-6-2T No. 69894. (R. Carpenter)

Opposite bottom: Another view of 69894 as it runs around its train before heading back to Darlington. (R. Carpenter)

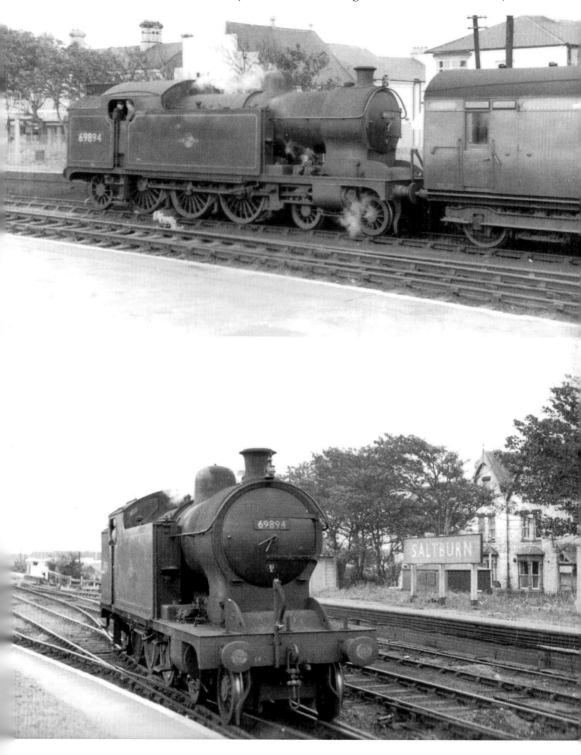

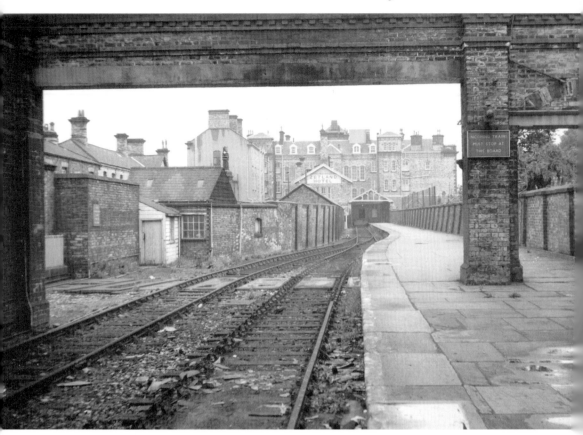

Saltburn station as it appeared in 1970, looking towards the dead end, with the Zetland Hotel beyond. In 1927, there was an accident between Saltburn and North Skelton when a train divided and the runaway portion was derailed. Fortunately, there were no casualties. (R. Casserley)

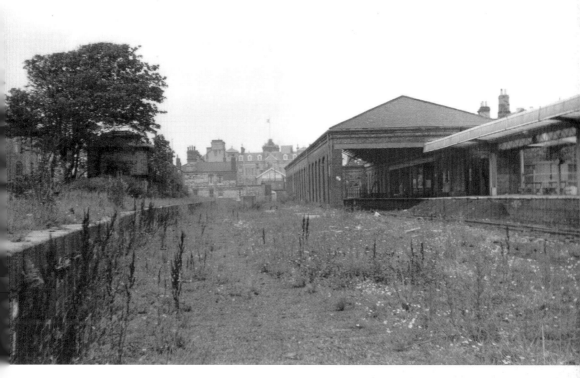

A view of the main station building and abandoned platform in 1970, a sign that rail traffic was in decline by this time. However, the station remains open to serve holiday and local traffic in the town. (R. Casserley)

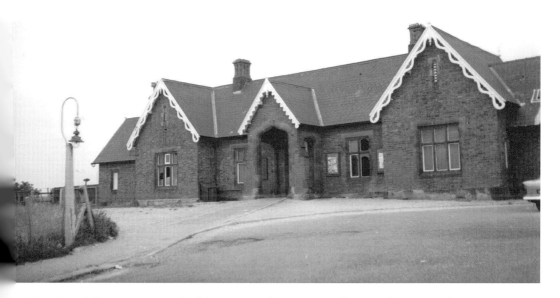

Exterior of the main station building at Marske in 1970. This was the intermediate station between Redcar and Saltburn when the extension opened in 1861. (R. Casserley)

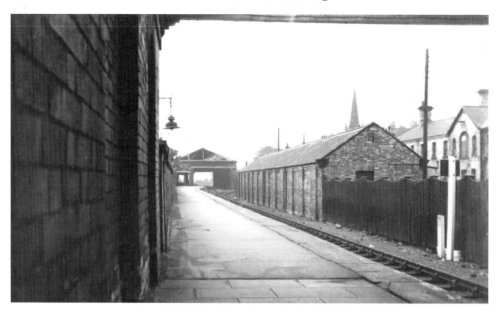

Saltburn station, looking from the dead end, and from the Zetland Hotel canopy, as it appeared on 20 August 1970. What appears to be the old loco shed is on the right. The shed here was approved in November 1863 and a tender of £411 13s 6d was accepted for a building to hold two locos. In February 1864 it was decided to have a shed for four engines, at a cost of a further £250. The shed was further extended in 1877 to hold six engines. On 17 April 1907, the roof was destroyed by fire, and Class 901 No. 853 was damaged. A new roof was erected later in the same year, and the two-road shed continued in use until 27 January 1958 when it closed, largely due to Darlington services being taken over by DMUs.

The shed was responsible for passenger trains working to Darlington and Scarborough. At 'Grouping', Darlington services were worked by Class D 4-4-4Ts (LNER Class H1) and Scarborough trains were operated by Class W (LNER Class A6) 4-6-2Ts, with two BTP 0-4-4Ts for autocar services. In May 1928, seven of Saltburn's Class H1s were exchanged for A5 4-6-2Ts from Blaydon and Gateshead due to unsatisfactory working of Class D engines on the Saltburn–Darlington line. In June 1930, the remaining two 4-4-4Ts at Saltburn went to Heaton. During March and April 1939, the A5s were replaced by seven A8 4-6-2Ts, all of which were rebuilds of H1 4-4-4Ts. Nine A8s were eventually allocated to Saltburn. The shed had three J24 0-6-0s – Nos 1860, 1893 and 1950 – in 1933 and also a Sentinel railcar, mainly used between Saltburn and Brotton. When the shed closed on 26 January 1958, all locos were transferred to Middlesbrough, although the yard continued in use to accommodate engines required to stand awaiting return excursions. The shed was finally demolished in 1960.

Allocation in 1949 was as follows:

Codes: LNER – S'BURN, BR – 51K.
J27 0-6-0   65857.
A5 4-6-2T   69831, 69834, 69842.
A8 4-6-2T   69869, 69876, 69883, 69884, 69889, 69891, 69892.
Total: 11.

Final allocation:

A5 4-6-2T   69830, 69831, 69834, 69842.
A8 4-6-2T   69866, 69869.
Total: 6. (R. Casserley)

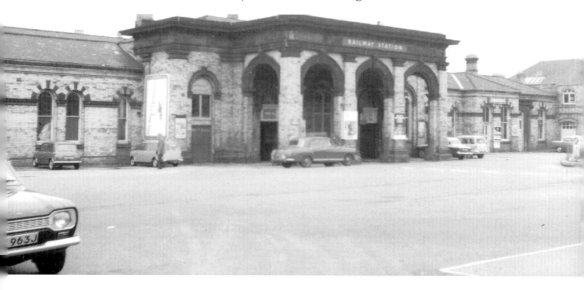

The exterior of Saltburn station, a rather handsome building, in 1970. Saltburn is probably unique on the North Yorkshire coast, because it is the only town to retain its Victorian pier. (R. Casserley)

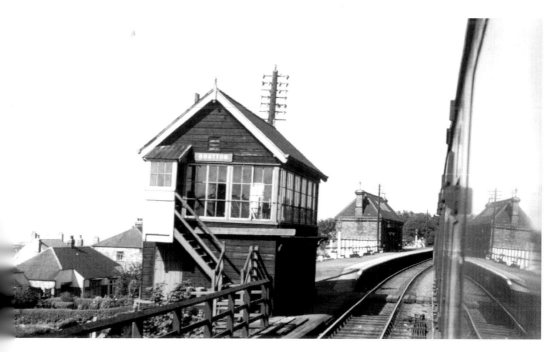

The signal box at Brotton, with the station beyond, on 1 September 1956, looking towards Whitby. This section, from Saltburn to Loftus, where it made a head-on connection with the line from Whitby, was built in the 1870s by the Cleveland Railway. The remainder of the route to Whitby was not opened until December 1883, due to construction difficulties. This Whitby line was short lived, closing on 5 May 1958, and the section from Loftus to Saltburn closed shortly afterwards. A section of the line between Redcar and Middlesbrough was reopened when ICI built Boulby potash mine just north of the village, and the line to the mine was connected with the old route. However, all of the stations remained closed. (H. Casserley)

Table 54 DARLINGTON, MIDDLESBROUGH and SALTBURN Bradshaw - April 1961

Week Days

(timetable columns – times for Darlington, Dinsdale, Eaglescliffe, Stockton, Eaglescliffe, Thornaby, Middlesbrough, Cargo Fleet, South Bank, Grangetown, Redcar Central, Redcar (East), Marske, Saltburn)

Week Days — continued

Sundays

Week Days

(Saltburn, Marske, Redcar (East), Redcar Central, Grangetown, South Bank, Cargo Fleet, Middlesbrough, Thornaby, Eaglescliffe, Stockton, Eaglescliffe, Dinsdale, Darlington)

Week Days — continued

Sundays

Sundays — continued

Notes:
a Through Carriages Saltburn to King's Cross (arr 5 20 am) via Stockton (Table 2) To Stockton arr 11 28 pm
B Connection at Thornaby
E or £ Except Saturdays
H Except Saturdays. Connection at Thornaby
Arr 8 32 pm on Fridays
RC Restaurant Car
N or S Saturdays only
T The Tees-Thames
TC Through Carriages
v Arr 5 39 am
: Arr 5 minutes *earlier* on Saturdays

For OTHER TRAINS between Thornaby and Middlesbrough, see Table 5

A timetable for April 1961, showing passenger services operating between Darlington, Middlesbrough and Saltburn. (Author's collection)

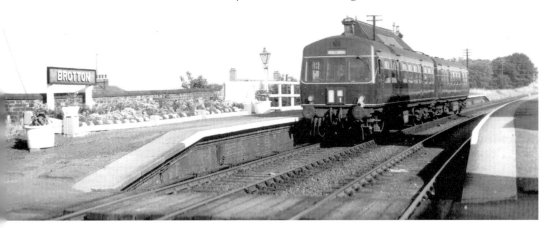

A sign of things to come, with a DMU working a Middlesbrough–Loftus service on 28 August 1958 at Brotton station. At Brotton on 15 February 1900 there was an accident when the driver of a train travelling at excessive speed passed a signal set at danger, causing a rear collision and derailment that resulted in nine injuries and one fatality. (H. Priestley)

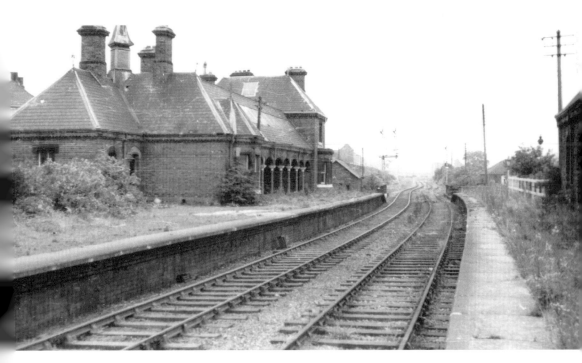

Brotton station, looking in the direction of Middlesbrough, in 1971. The main station building and the platform appear to be in a neglected state. (R. Casserley)

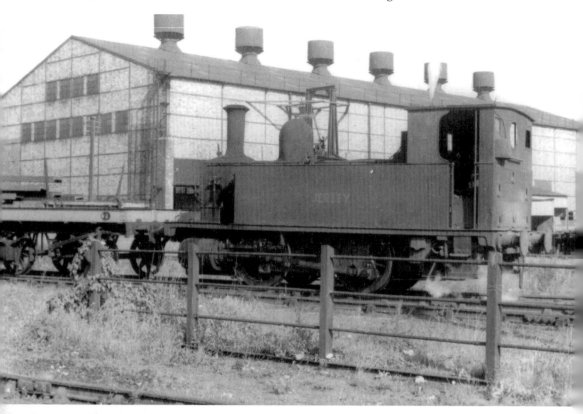

Beyond Brotton there was a station at Carlin How, which was provided with a loco shed, built in January 1866, after a tender of £1,261 13s was accepted, to accommodate mineral engines; in 1885 ex-S&DR long-boilered 0-6-0s were allocated here for working ironstone traffic to blast furnaces at Teesside. There were also Class 1037 0-6-0Ts for shunting duties and one BTP 0-4-4T, which replaced an ex-S&DR 2-4-0, for Loftus–Middlesbrough services. The shed closed on 1 October 1902, reopened in March 1907 and finally closed in 1921, the building surviving until 1954. Near to Carlin How was Skinningrove steelworks, seen here on 28 August 1958 with an ex-LSWR/SR B4 Class 0-4-0, as No. 81 *Jersey*, which had been purchased by the steelworks. (R. Carpenter collection)

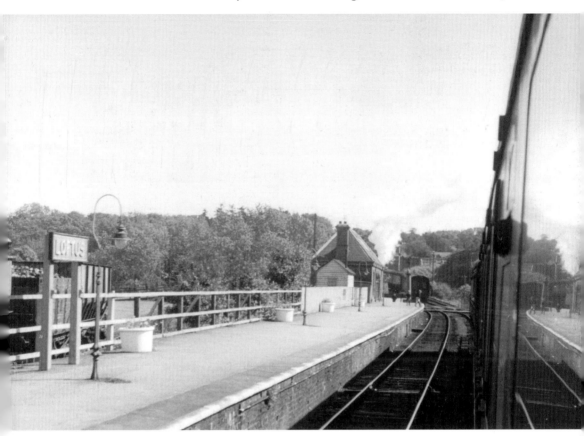

The point at which the Cleveland Railway met the line from Whitby at Loftus. The station is seen here on 1 September 1956. (H. Casserley)

Up.		mrn	mrn	mrn	mrn	mrn	aft	aft	aft	aft	aft	aft	aft
...burn ....dep.		....	6 40	8 4	9 3	1121	1255	....	....	4 20	....	6 21	
...th Skelton		....	6 51	8 15	9 14	1131	1 6	....	....	4 30	....	6 31	
...tton	arr.	....	6 55	....	9 18	1135	....	....	....	4 35	....	....	
	dep.	....	6 58	....	9 22	1138	....	2 30	....	4 38	....	....	
...sbeck		....	7 5	8 21	9 29	1145	1 12	2 37	....	4 45	....	6 37	
...sborough	arr.	....	7 15	8 33	9 39	1155	1 22	2 47	....	4 55	....	6 46	
	dep.	5 17	7 23	8 37	9 42	12 1	1 24		3 23	5 1	6 0	6 48	10 8
...ton Gate		5 21	7 27	8 41	9 46	12 5	1 28		3 27	5 5	6 4	6 52	1012
...hingthorpe		5 25	7 31	8 45	9 50	12 9	1 32		3 31	5 9	6 8	6 56	1016
...thorpe 719		5 31	7 37	8 51	9 56	1215	1 38		3 37	5 15	6 14	7 2	1022
...esby		5 35	7 41	8 55	10 0	1219	1 42		3 41	5 19	6 18	7 6	1026
...dlesbrough *(see above)*/ar		5 42	7 48	9 2	10 7	1226	1 49		3 48	5 26	6 25	7 13	1033

SALTBURN, GUISBOROUGH, and MIDDLESBROUGH (Auto-cars).—North Eastern.

Week Days.

(column marked "Sats. only."; final column marked "Weds. and Sats.")

☞ For other Trains

BETWEEN PAGE
Saltburn and Brotton 718
Nunthorpe and Middlesbrough 719

A 1910 timetable for trains from Saltburn, Guisborough and Middlesbrough, which were operated as autotrain services. (Author's collection)

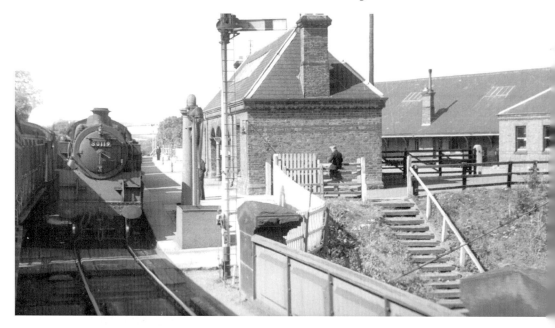

On the same day, BR 'Standard' Class 4 2-6-4T No. 80119 waits at Loftus station with the 12.37 p.m. service from Middlesbrough to Whitby. (H. Casserley)

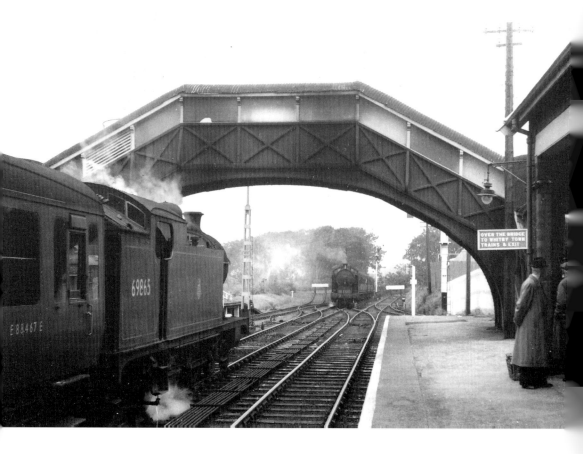

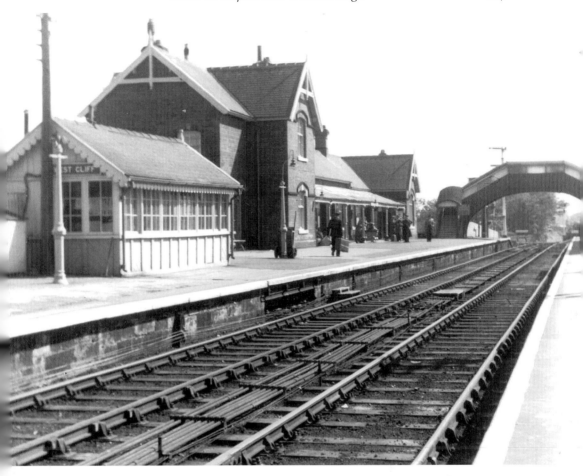

From Loftus, the line continued along the Whitby, Redcar & Middlesbrough Union Railway until arriving at Whitby West Cliff station, seen here on 1 September 1956, from where a shuttle train connected the station with Whitby Town. (R. Casserley)

A pair of ex-LNER Class A8 4-6-2Ts at Whitby West Cliff in September 1957. The nearest, No. 69865, is about to depart with a train for Scarborough, while No. 69885 is approaching with a train for Saltburn. (R. Carpenter)

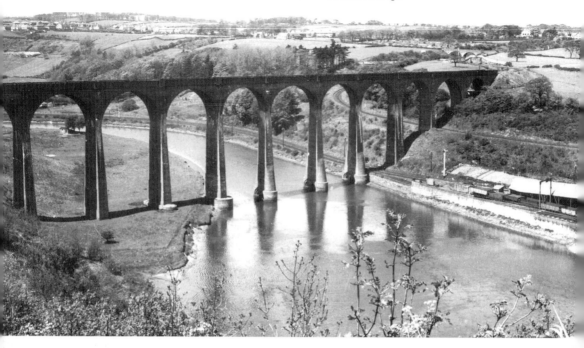

After departing from West Cliff and heading towards Scarborough, the line crossed Larpool Viaduct, seen here in the 1950s. Below is the Esk Valley line between Whitby Town and Grosmont, along with the connecting line between West Cliff and Whitby Town. (R. Carpenter collection)

Opposite top: The terminus of the line from Middlesbrough, Loftus and Whitby was at Scarborough, seen here early in the twentieth century with NER Class M1 (later LNER Class D17) 4-4-0 No. 1629, built in 1893, at the head of a train from York. (Author's collection)

Opposite bottom: A 1930s view of the platforms at Scarborough station, with a pair of Sentinel railcars departing with a local service to Pickering. On the left, an express to York is about to leave. (LOSA)

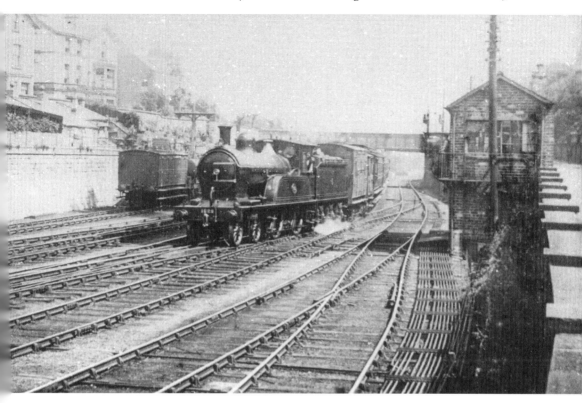

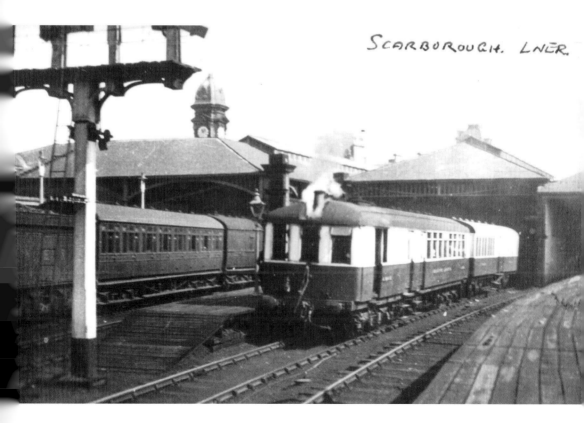

SCARBOROUGH. LNER.

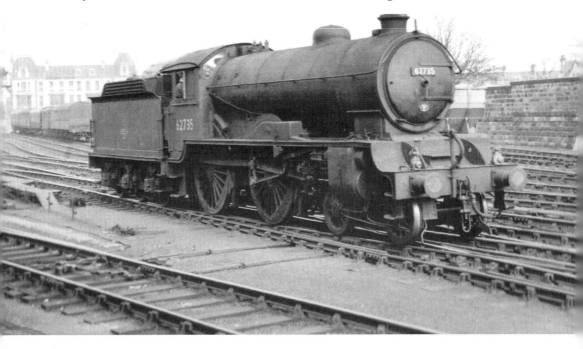

Standing just outside Scarborough station is ex-LNER Class D49 4-4-0 No. 62735 *Westmorland* on 30 April 1958. (R. Carpenter)

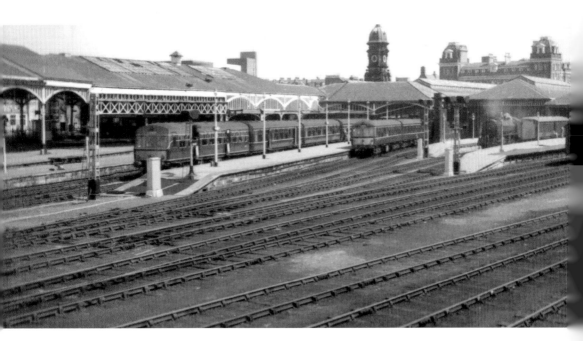

Another view of ex-LNER B1 4-6-0, No. 61319, on shunting duties during the summer of 1965. By this time, DMUs had taken over most traffic from Scarborough, as can be seen here. (R. Carpenter collection)

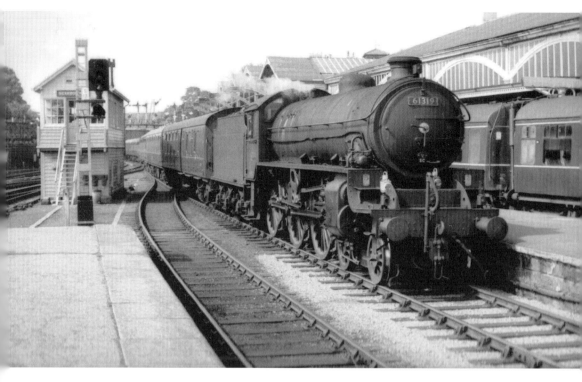

During the summer of 1965, ex-LNER Class B1 4-6-0 No. 61319 is seen approaching the buffer stops with empty coaching stock. (R. Carpenter collection)

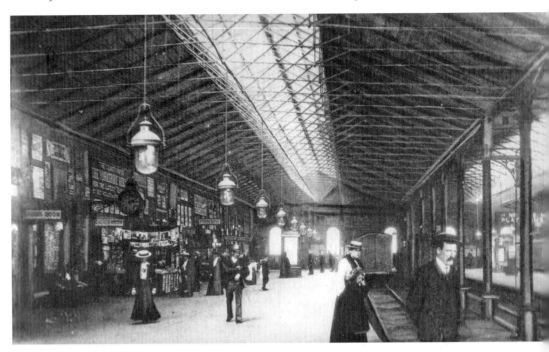

The interior of the terminus at Scarborough station when it was operated by the NER at the end of the nineteenth century. (LOSA)

Opposite top: Back at Brotton, the line to Boosbeck, for Guisborough and Nunthorpe, left the Saltburn–Loftus route, as seen here on 1 September 1956. (H. Casserley)

Opposite bottom: The first station on the line was at Boosbeck, seen here, facing Whitby, in 1956. (R. Casserley)

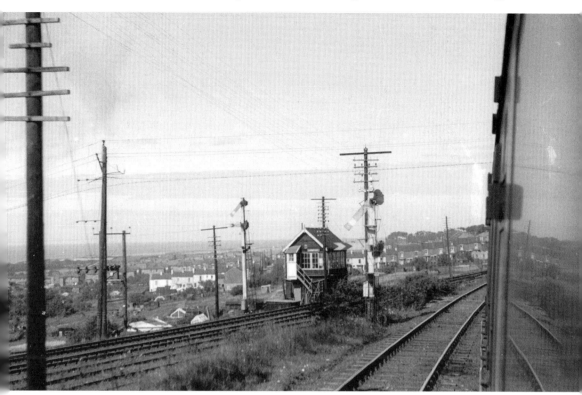

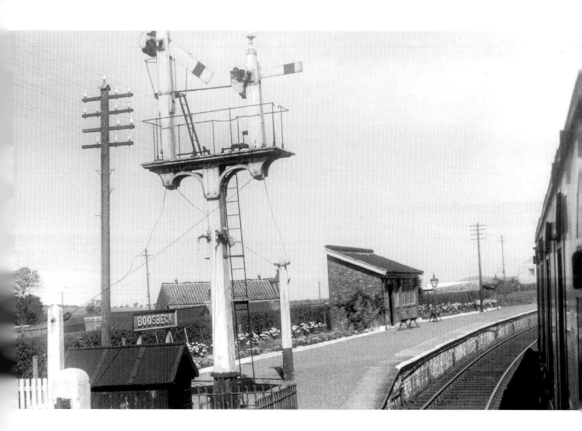

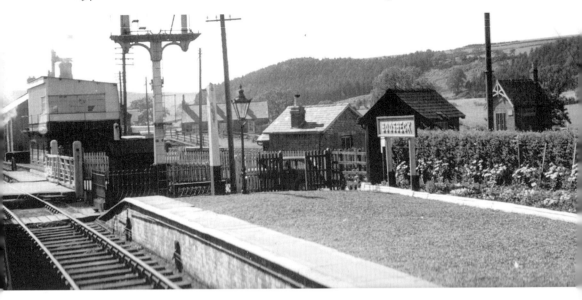

Another view of Boosbeck station in 1956, looking towards Middlesbrough. (H. Casserley)

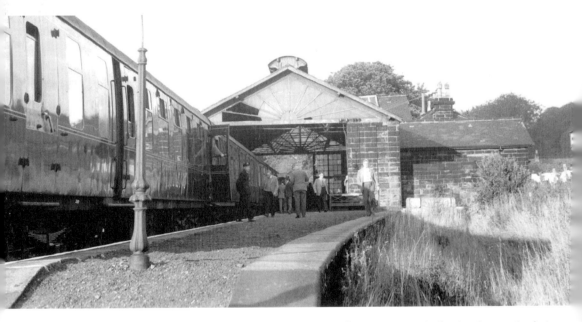

The terminus station at Guisborough on 30 September 1963, a train having just arrived. As the NER had connected the Cleveland Railway line to the M&G east of Guisborough, trains had to reverse out of the terminus before continuing along the line to Loftus and Saltburn. This arrangement continued until the whole line closed in 1960. (H. Casserley)

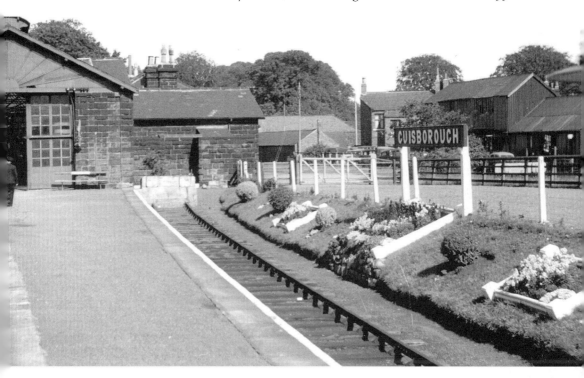

Looking towards the dead end at Guisborough station in 1956, showing the main building and overall roof. Guisborough was also supplied with a loco shed, which was opened along with the M&G in 1853. This building was destroyed by fire on 27 February 1903, and replaced some five years later by a corrugated iron structure that lasted until final closure on 20 September 1954. Coded G'BORO by the LNER and 51D (a sub-shed of Middlesbrough) by BR, the shed supplied autotrain locos for services to Middlesbrough, Saltburn and Loftus. In NER days, BTP 0-4-4Ts operated such services but, by 1929, these engines were disappearing and, on 29 July, an F8 2-4-2T, No. 685, was transferred from Middlesbrough to replace the last BTP. In November of the following year, Guisborough lost its loco and acquired a Sentinel steam railcar, *Old Blue*. The railcar was scrapped in 1941 and, on 15 September 1941, G5 0-4-4T No. 1883 replaced it. It was one of the first of the class fitted with the LNMER pattern of push-pull apparatus, and it remained at Guisborough, as BR No. 67281, until the shed finally closed. (H. Casserley)

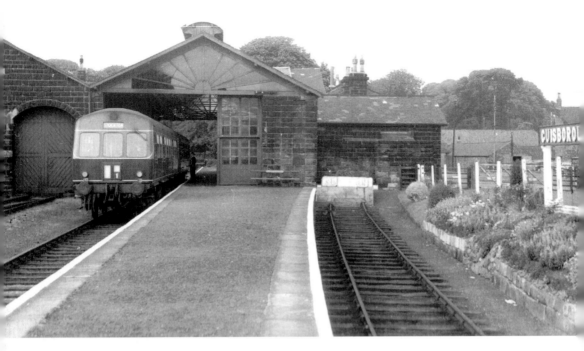

The replacements for steam autotrains on services at Guisborough were DMUs, as seen here on 27 August 1958. (R. Carpenter collection)

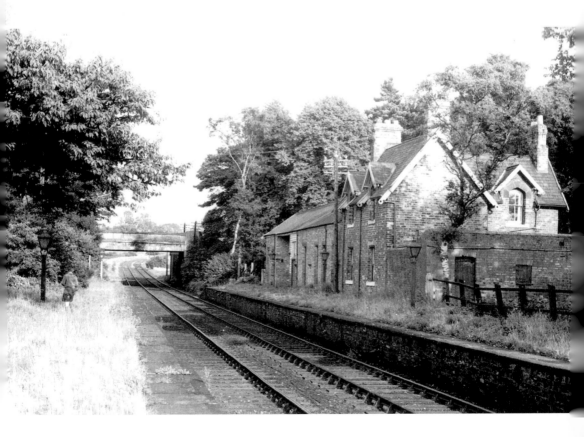

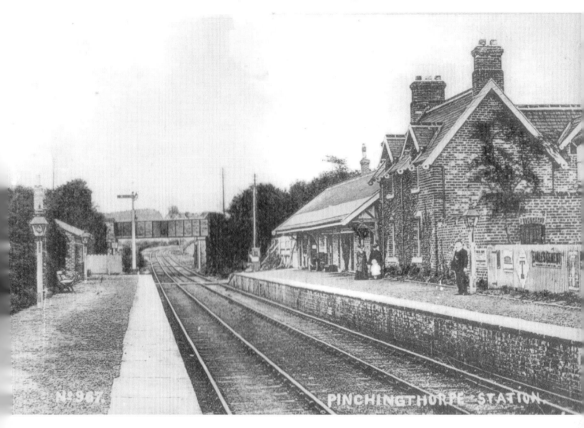

Pinchinthorpe station in NER days. A station here was opened in 1904, and nearby Hutton Gate was bought by the railway company for public use. (LOSA)

Opposite bottom: Another view of Pinchinthorpe station in 1958. The station looks in a derelict state, which is not surprising as it was closed in 1951, after a working life of less than fifty years. (R. Carpenter collection)

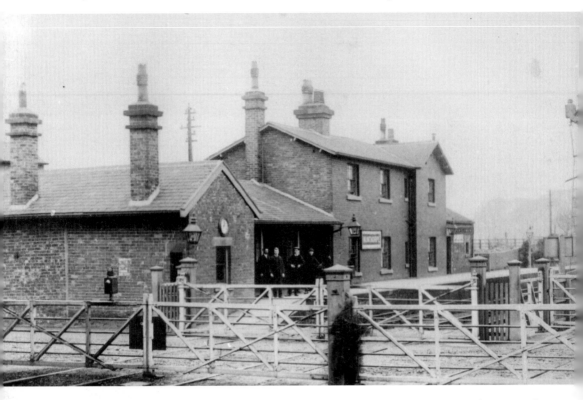

Nunthorpe station building and level crossing early in the twentieth century. The station here was a junction with the M&G and Esk Valley line to Battersby, via Great Ayton. (LOSA)

Opposite top: Nunthorpe station, facing Guisborough, as it appeared on 2 June 1935. The line from Nunthorpe Junction to Guisborough was closed in 1964, which left the section from Middlesbrough to Battersby open, Nunthorpe then losing its junction status. Nunthorpe station itself is now part of the Esk Valley line from Middlesbrough to Whitby. (H. Casserley)

Opposite bottom: Exterior of the station at Ormesby, showing the overbridge and roadway. In steam days, this was the only station between Nunthorpe and Middlesbrough on the M&G. But after the line to Guisborough was closed and the Tees valley network had been created, Ormesby station was renamed Marton to take advantage of James Cook connections, and a new station, closer to Nunthorpe, was opened and named Gypsy Lane. (LOSA)

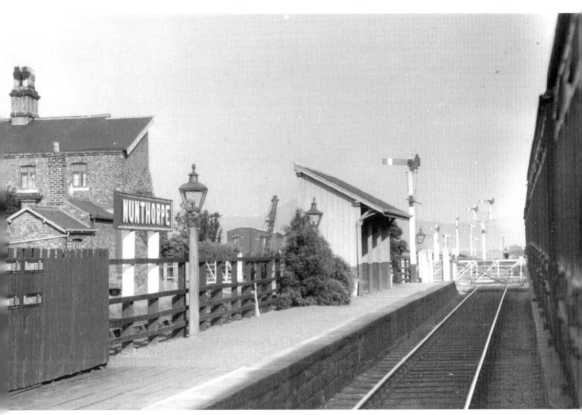

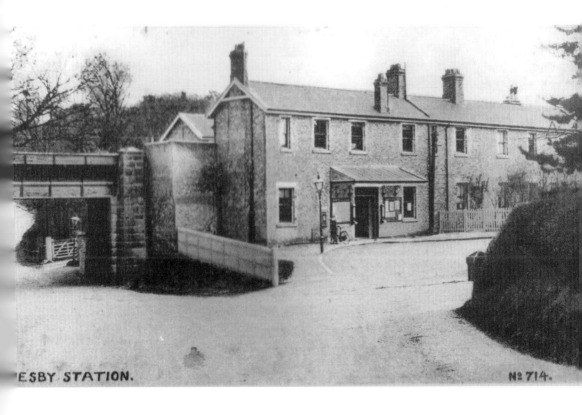

ESBY STATION. No 714.

MIDDLESBROUGH, GUISBOROUGH, and SALTBURN (Auto-cars).—North Eastern.

Miles	Down.		mrn	mrn	mrn	mrn	aft	aft	aft	aft	aft	aft	aft	aft		aft		For of Trains
	Middlesbrough ....dep.		6 20	8 40	9 42	1157	1251		2 47	4 52	5 17	6 0	8 20	....		1048	....	
3	Ormesby		6 27	8 47	9 49	12 4	1258	Sats. only.	2 54	4 59	5 24	6 7	8 27	....	Weds. and Sats.	1055	....	
4½	Nunthorpe		6 33	8 53	9 55	1210	1 4		3 0	5 5	5 30	6 13	8 33	....		11 1	....	
7¼	Pinchingthorpe...........		6 39	8 59	10 1	1216	1 10		3 6	5 11	5 36	6 19	8 39	....		11 7	....	
8¾	Hutton Gate		6 43	9 3	10 5	1220	1 14		3 10	5 15	5 40	6 23	8 43	....		1111	....	Trains
10	Guisborough ....{arr.	6 47	9 7	10 9	1224	1 18		3 14	5 19	5 44	6.27	8 47	....		1115	....	BETWEEN
10	{dep.	6 49	9 10	1011	1226	....	1 45	3 16	5 21	....	....	....	8 54		....	....	Middlesbrough a... Nunthorpe....
14	Boosbeck		6 59	9 20	1021	1236	....	1 55	3 26	5 31	....	....	....	9 7		....	....	Brotton and Sa... burn ....
16¾	Brotton 718 ....{arr.	7 4	9 26	....	....	....	2 0	3 31	5 36	....	....	....	9 12		....	....	
16¾	{dep.	....	....	....	....	....	....	3 37	5 42	....	....	....	9 18		....	....	
18¼	North Skelton...........		....	....	1026	....	....	....	3 41	5 46	....	....	....	9 22		....	....	
21	Saltburn 707..........arr.		....	....	1038	1247	....	....	3 53	5 58	....	....	....	9 35		....	....	

A NER timetable for autotrain services between Middlesbrough and Saltburn, along the M&G and Cleveland railway lines. (Author's collection)

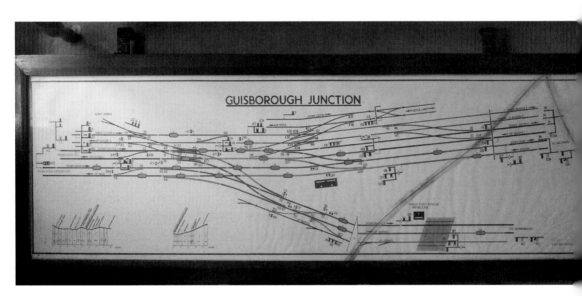

The signalling diagram for the box that controlled Guisborough Junction; the line to Guisborough left the main Middlesbrough–Saltburn line at this point. (Paul Hughes collection)

THE ESK VALLEY LINE

Built by the North Yorkshire & Cleveland Railway, the section of railway between Picton, on the Leeds Northern Railway from Northallerton to Eaglescliffe, and Battersby connected with the section from Battersby to Grosmont, where it joined the line to Whitby and the branch to Pickering, which itself connected with the main Scarborough–York line. Stations on the section from Picton were at Trenholme Bar, Potto, Sexhow, Stokesley and Ingleby, all closing to passengers in 1954. Goods trains running south from Battersby to Ingleby were raised on a cable pulley system up a steep incline and across moors to iron-ore workings at Rosedale and Ferndale. A loco shed was opened at Rosedale in 1861, and had four 0-6-0s, two built by Robert Stephenson & Co. in 1860 and the others built by R. & W. Hawthorn & Co. in 1866. From 1903 to 1920, ex-S&DR long-boilered 0-6-0s were in use. These engines were used to haul wagons of ironstone from mines at East and West Rosedale to Incline Top, where wagons were lowered down the incline and taken forward by another engine. At the top, the engine worked empty wagons back to the mines. There was a small amount of general freight traffic, but this was insignificant when compared with ironstone traffic. The shed was demolished in the 1930s and the stone was used to build the village hall at Hutton-le-Hole, some 4 miles away.

Between Glaisdale and Lealholm, one John Waddell began working on a branch across the moors to access iron-ore mines in the area. The plan was to meet the Guisborough line near Boulby, but a collapse of ore prices meant that the route was never finished.

The Picton–Grosmont section was connected to the Middlesbrough–Guisborough line by a branch, built in 1864, from Nunthorpe to Battersby. This section is still in use today as the Esk Valley line, as it runs between Middlesbrough and Whitby, the only railway access to this isolated seaside resort.

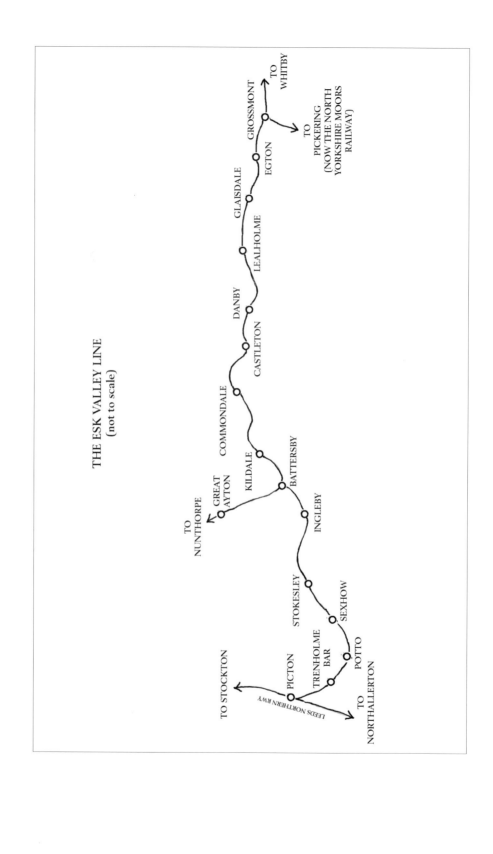

THE ESK VALLEY LINE
(not to scale)

TO WHITBY

GROSSMONT

TO PICKERING
(NOW THE NORTH
YORKSHIRE MOORS
RAILWAY)

EGTON

GLAISDALE

LEALHOLME

DANBY

CASTLETON

COMMONDALE

KILDALE

BATTERSBY

GREAT AYTON

TO NUNTHORPE

INGLEBY

STOKESLEY

SEXHOW

TRENHOLME BAR

POTTO

PICTON

LEEDS NORTHERN RWY

TO STOCKTON

TO NORTHALLERTON

WHITBY, BATTERSBY, and STOCKTON.—North Eastern.

Up. — Week Days.

Town Station.	mrn	mrn	mrn	aft	aft	aft
Whitby ....dep.	7 0	...	1011	1 30	3 5	5 50
Ruswarp	7 5	...	1016	1 35	3 10	5 55
Sleights	7 10	...	1021	1 40	3 15	6 0
Grosmont	7 20	...	1030	1 51	3 24	6 9
Egton	7 25	...	1035	1 56	3 29	6 14
Glaisdale	7 30	...	1040	2 3	3 34	6 19
Lealholm	7 36	...	1046	2 9	3 40	6 25
Danby	7 44	...	1054	2 17	3 48	6 33
Castleton	7 48	...	1058	2 21	3 52	6 27
Commondale	7 53	...	11 3	2 26	3 57	6 42
Kildale	8 2	...	1112	2 35	4 6	6 51
Battersby 719 arr.	8 6	...	1115	2 38	4 9	6 54
19 MIDDLESBRO' arr.	8 40	...	1154	3 26	5 33	7 34
Battersby dep.	8 10	8 11	1119	2 46	4 13	6 58
Ingleby		8 14	Sig.	2 49	4 16	7 1
Stokesley		8 21	1127	2 56	4 22	7 8
Sexhow		8 28	1134	3 3	4 28	7 15
Potto		8 32	1138	3 7	4 32	7 19
Trenholme Bar		8 39	1144	3 13	4 38	7 25
Picton 710		8 46	1149	3 19	4 44	7 31
Yarm		8 53	1155	3 26	4 50	7 38
Eaglescliffe arr./dep.		8 59	1158	3 30	4 54	7 41
Stockton 708 arr.		9 1	12 3	3 34	4 57	7 46
		8 59	7 12	9 3	40 5	5 7	52
92 NEWCASTLE (C.) arr.	1012	1055	1 54	5c25	6 38	9c58

Down. — Week Days.

Miles	Central Station.	mrn	mrn	mrn	aft	aft	aft	aft
	692 NEWCASTLE..dep.	5 10	3 30	...	1230c	2c40	...	4 20	5 53
—	Stockton....dep.	7 38	1030	...	1 52	...	4 10	5 35	8 12
3	Eaglescliffe arr./dep.	7 44	1036	...	1 58	...	4 16	5 41	8 18
4½	Yarm	7 48	1038	...	2 1	...	4 20	5 51	8 21
7½	Picton	7 52	1042	...	2 5	...	4 24	5 56	8 25
9½	Trenholme Bar	8 0	1050	...	2 13	...	4 32	6 5	8 33
12	Potto	8 6	1056	...	2 19	...	4 38	6 11	8 39
13	Sexhow	8 11	11 1	...	2 24	...	4 43	6 16	8 44
16½	Stokesley	8 15	11 5	...	2 28	...	4 47	6 20	8 48
19½	Ingleby	8 22	1112	...	2 35	...	4 54	6 28	8 55
19½	Battersby 719 arr.	8 29	1119	...	2 42	...	5 0	Sig. 9 2
	719 MIDDLESBRO' dep.	7 30	...	1045	2 13	...	4 32	8 32
	Battersby dep.	8 32	1122	...	2 45	...	5 3	6 38	9 5
	Battersby ......dep.	8 36	1130	2 53	...	5 10	9 9
21¼	Kildale	8 41	1135	2 58	...	5 15	9 14
25½	Commondale	8 49	1143	3 7	...	5 23	9 22
27¼	Castleton	8 54	1148	3 12	...	5 28	9 27
28½	Danby	8 59	1153	3 17	...	5 33	9 32
32½	Lealholm	9 5	1159	3 24	...	5 39	9 38
34½	Glaisdale	9 10	12 4	3 29	3 35	5 44	9 43
36	Egton	9 15	12 9		3 40	5 49	9 48
37½	Grosmont 720	9 20	1214		3 45	5 57	9 53
40½	Sleights	9 29	1223		3 54	6 7	10 3
42¾	Ruswarp	9 33	1227		3 58	6 11	10 7
43¼	Whitby (Town)	9 40	1234		4 5	6 18	10 14

ç Via Darlington.

A 1910 NER timetable for trains between Whitby, Battersby, Middlesbrough, Picton (on the Leeds Northern line), Eaglescliffe and Stockton. (Author's collection)

Opposite: A map of the Esk Valley line between Picton and Grosmont, where it made a junction with the line from Whitby to Pickering (the section from Grosmont to Pickering is now the North Yorkshire Moors Railway). As can be seen, Battersby was also a junction with a line from here to Nunthorpe, the only intermediate station being at Great Ayton. The modern service between Whitby and Middlesbrough uses this route, and the NYMR also operates steam trains between Pickering and the seaside town over the Esk Valley line from Grosmont. (Author)

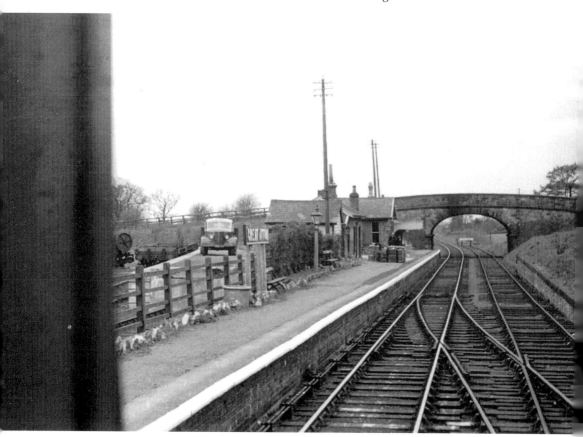

Great Ayton station, looking towards Middlesbrough, as it appeared on 27 April 1954. The branch was built in 1864 to connect the Picton–Grosmont line with the Middlesbrough–Guisborough route, and ran through to Nunthorpe Junction. As previously mentioned, this is the only station between Battersby and Nunthorpe and remains as part of the modern Esk Valley line from Middlesbrough to Whitby. (R. Casserley)

Opposite bottom: Battersby station on 27 April 1953, with the 1.22 p.m. service to Whitby having just arrived, hauled by ex-LNER Class A8 4-6-2T No. 69861. (R. Casserley)

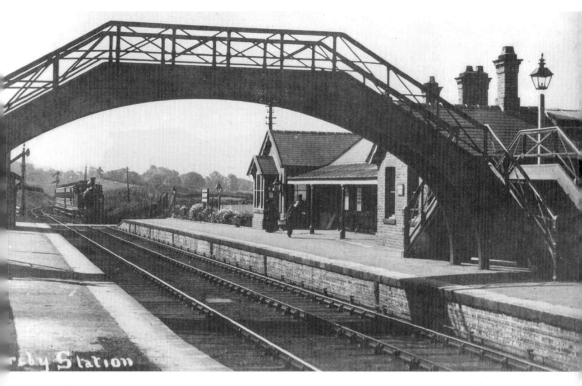

Battersby station as it appeared in NER days, with a local train arriving at the station. The station is situated on the line from Picton, where it joined the Leeds Northern line from Northallerton to Eaglescliffe, and was built by the North Yorkshire & Cleveland Railway, which itself was absorbed into the NER in 1858. The section between Castleton and Battersby was opened to mineral traffic as far as Battersby on 6 April 1858, to take advantage of traffic from ironstone mines at Ingleby, no doubt. Passenger services from Stokesley to Castleton commenced on 1 April 1861. The section between Picton and Battersby closed to passengers in 1954. (LOSA)

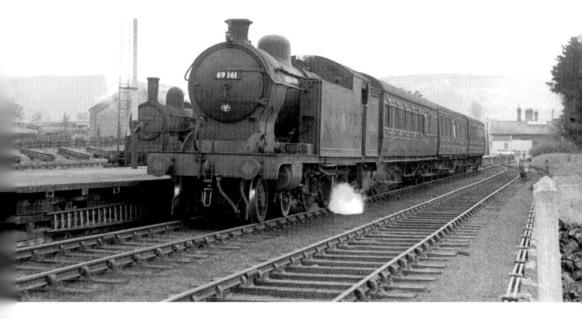

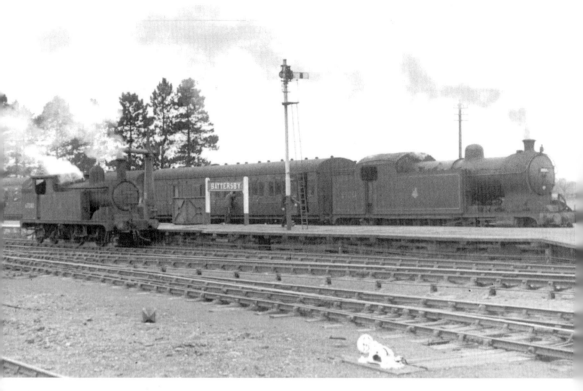

On the same day, ex-NER G5 0-4-4T No. 67343 is waiting to run round its train, while No. 69861 prepares to depart for Whitby. (R. Casserley)

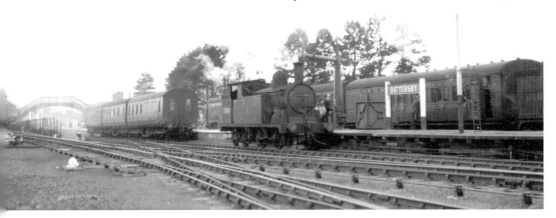

Running round the 12 noon Stockton–Battersby local service, which ran via Picton, is ex-NER G5 0-4-4T, No. 67343, in the last year that passenger services ran over the line to Picton. (H. Casserley)

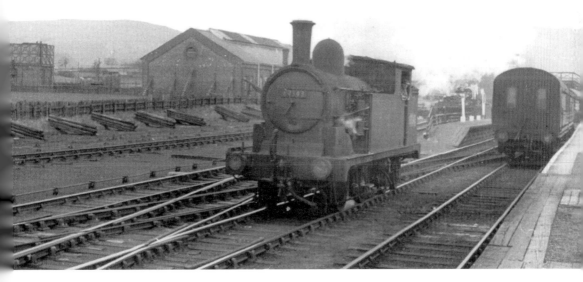

No. 67343 as seen from the platform at Battersby on 27 April 1954, looking in the direction of Picton. The line to Picton has ceased to exist, and only a small section runs past the station and around the bend where it ends. (R. Casserley)

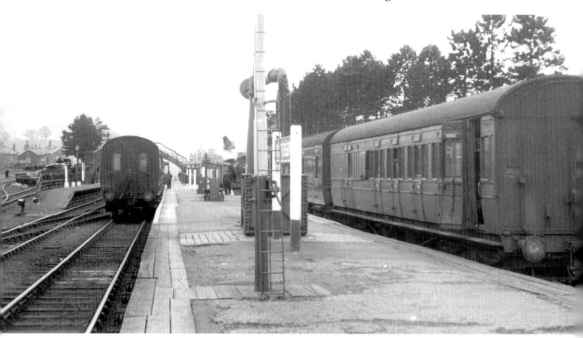

Rolling stock at Battersby in 1954. Freight trains ran through Battersby, south to Ingleby, where wagons were hauled up a rope incline for iron ore workings at Rosedale. Here, freight engines would haul wagons to and from the mines. Rosedale and Battersby had several Class 1001 'Long Boiler' 0-6-0 engines for such work. The design dated back to the S&DR, whose engineer, William Bouch, had designed these locos, which were built at Shildon, although some were constructed by private contractors, in 1846 for use on heavy freight trains from the West Auckland coalfields. Their long boilers acted as a steam reservoir, which was required to restart heavy trains; these trains were often delayed in sidings to allow faster ones to pass. The NER continued to build further examples, which eventually numbered 192, the last being retired by the LNER in February 1923. By the 1890s, these locos tended to be concentrated in the Darlington area, a handful operating out of Rosedale to operate the heavy ironstone trains from the mines in the area and along the line around Battersby. To accommodate engines to work stone trains from Ingleby incline, Battersby was provided with a loco shed, which had been authorised on 17 December 1874. The proposal was for a shed to be built that could house eight locos, together with thirty cottages to be built at Ingleby, and a tender of £2,500 1s 4d was accepted on 6 May 1875, the shed opening in 1877. The shed was closed a few years later due to a decline in iron ore traffic, but reopened on 1 December 1889, only to close again on 30 November 1895, only four engines being stationed there at that time. (H. Casserley)

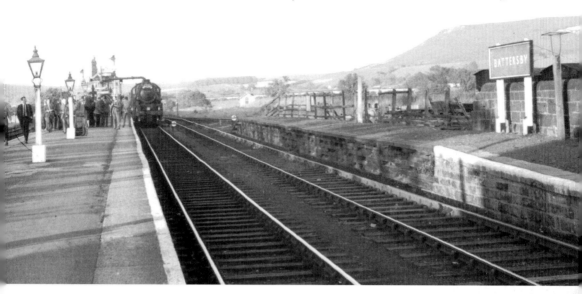

Ex-LMS Ivatt Class 4 2-6-0 No. 43129 waits at Battersby station with an enthusiasts' special from Whitby on 30 September 1963. A crowd of enthusiasts watch as the loco takes on water before continuing its journey. (H. Casserley)

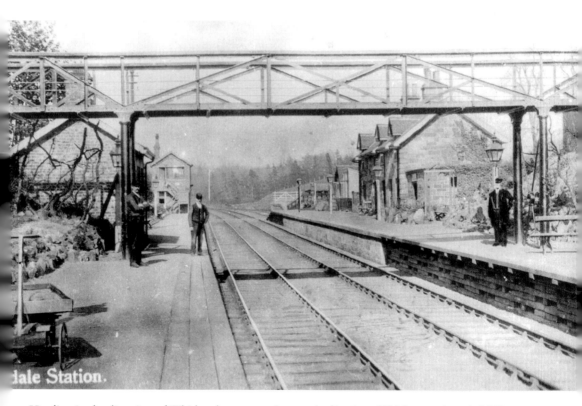

Heading in the direction of Whitby, the next station on the line is at Kildale, seen here in NER days with staff and passengers in view. (LOSA)

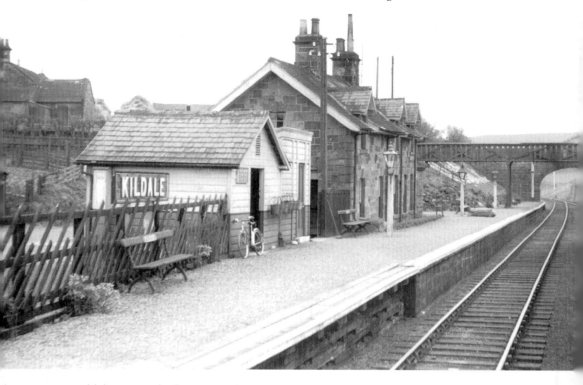

Kildale station, looking towards Battersby, as it appeared on 27 April 1954. Like all of the stations on the line between Whitby and Nunthorpe, it remains open to serve passengers along the route. (H. Casserley)

Opposite top: Commondale station, looking back in the direction of Battersby, as it appeared in April 1954. (R. Casserley)

Opposite bottom: Danby station on the Castleton–Grosmont section, as it appeared in NER days. This section was the last to be completed and it was opened on 2 October 1865 to complete the whole route from Picton to Whitby. (LOSA)

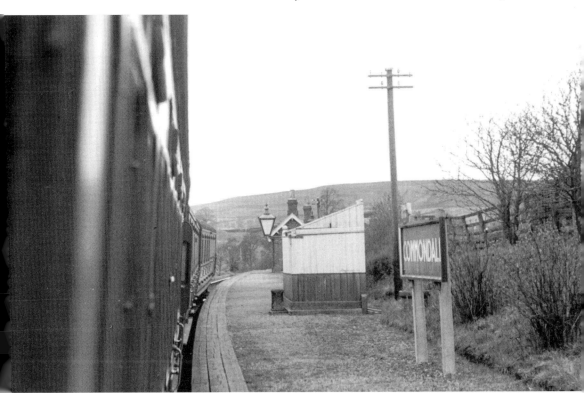

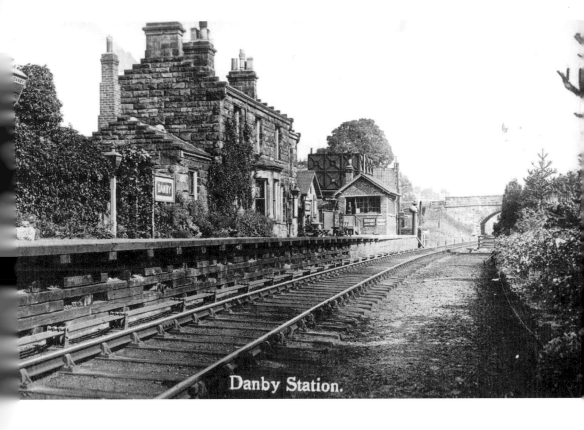

Danby Station.

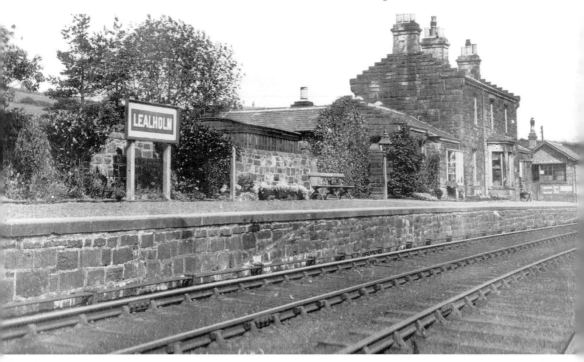

From Danby, the next station is at Lealholm, seen here in NER days. Between here and Glaisdale, work was started by railway engineer John Wadell on a branch across the moors to take advantage of iron ore traffic in the area. It was intended that the line would meet the Guisborough line near Boulby. A collapse in iron ore prices meant that the line was never completed, and earthworks, which would have formed cuttings and embankments, can be seen at various points along the route. This line was to have one intermediate station at Stonegate and a tunnel, which would have been constructed using the 'cut and cover' method. Only one bridge was completed, at Rake Farm, between Lealholm and Glaisdale, at the junction with the Esk Valley line. (LOSA)

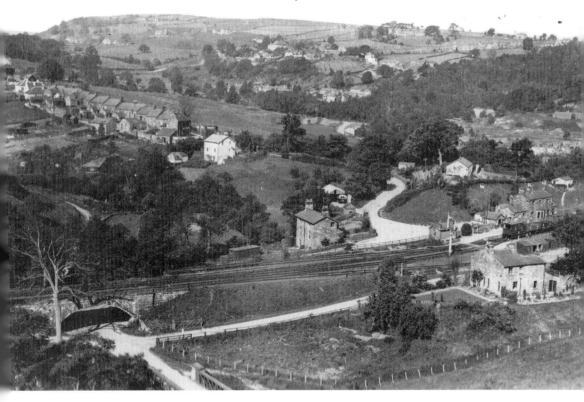

An aerial view of the station at Glaisdale, with a pick-up goods train waiting at the station. The village is visible beyond the station, with hills and farmland behind, all of which brought revenue to the NER. (LOSA)

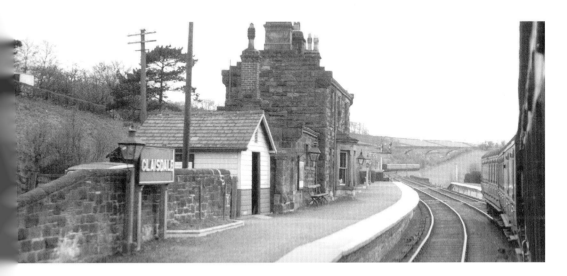

The main building, in typical NER style, as it appeared in April 1954, looking in the direction of Battersby. (H. Casserley)

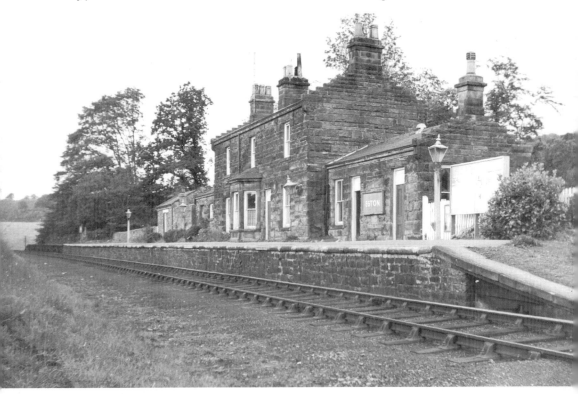

From Glaisdale, the next station on the way to Whitby is at Egton, seen here on 16 August 1970, showing the NER stone-built main building. (R. Casserley)

Opposite top: Egton station in 1954, looking back toward Battersby. (R. Casserley)

Opposite bottom: The junction station at Grosmont as it appeared on 1 September 1956. The line to Pickering, which is now the NYMR, is on the left, and the line to Battersby and Middlesbrough is on the right. Back in the days before the line to Pickering was closed by BR, the branch ran past Pickering and on to the main Scarborough–York line, via Marishes Road (the old station still exists here) to Rillington and Malton, where connections could be made to King's Cross, via York, Scarborough and along rural branches to Driffield, where connections could be made for Hull and Bridlington. From Grosmont, the Esk Valley line will run down to Whitby, via Sleights and Ruswarp. (H. Casserley)

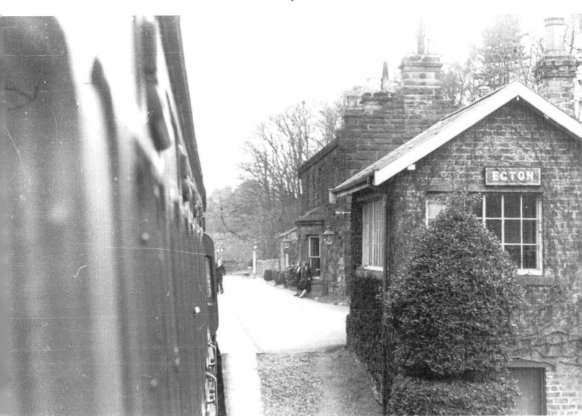

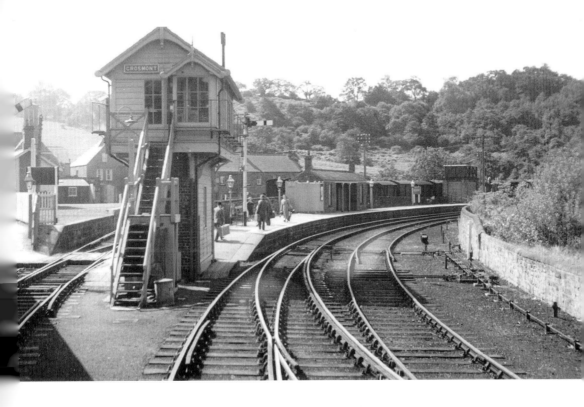

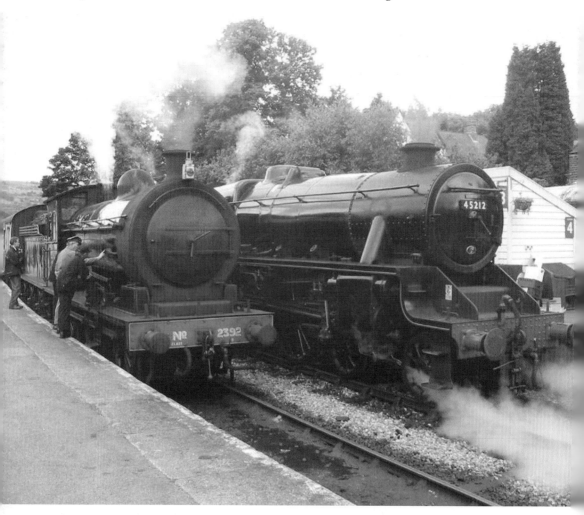

Pictured at Grosmont station in 2007 is an ex-LNER Class J27 0-6-0, BR No. 65894, seen here in NER livery as No. 2392; the engine was actually built in 1923 under LNER auspices. These engines were a familiar sight on goods trains in the Middlesbrough area and the North East in general. Next to the NER loco is ex-LMS Stanier Black Five 4-6-0 No. 45212, which will take the train back to Pickering. Closure by BR of the line between Rillington and Grosmont occurred in 1965, and two years later, meetings formed the North York Moors Railway Preservation Society and the line reopened in 1969, passenger trains operating between Grosmont and Goathland on 22 April 1973. Since then, the line has gone from strength to strength, helped, no doubt, by use of the railway for the television series *Heartbeat*, the TV company filming many scenes at Goathland station. (J. Thurston)

Opposite top: Resting at Grosmont station, after bringing in a train from Whitby, is ex-Southern Railway Schools Class 4-4-0 No. 30926 *Repton* during the summer of 2012. The NYMR has a collection of locomotives from all four of the 'Grouping' companies, as well as examples of BR Standard engines. (Author)

Opposite bottom: Waiting at Grosmont station is an ex-BR Standard Class 4, 2-6-0 No. 76079, as it waits for its turn of duty to Pickering. (J. Thurston)

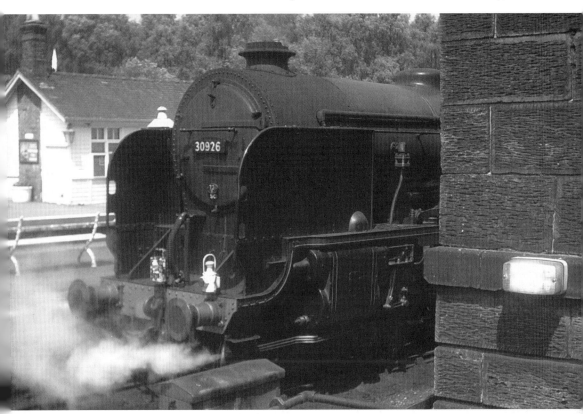

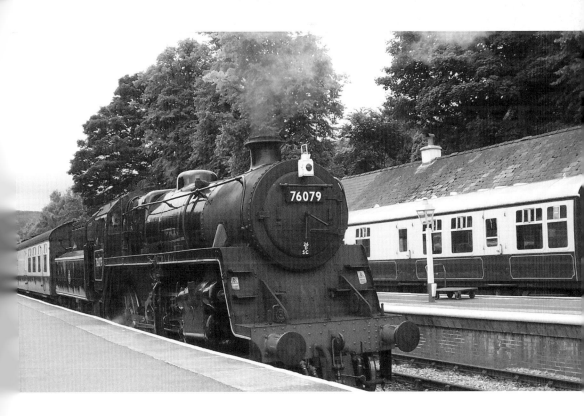

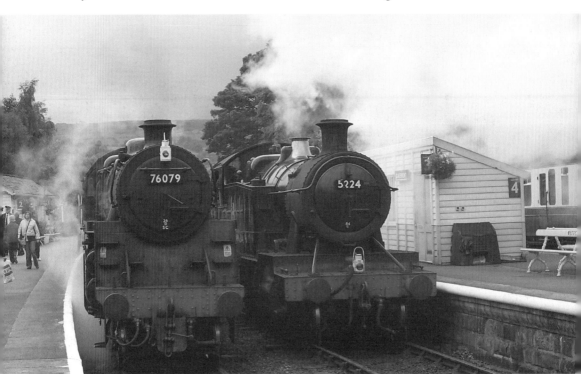

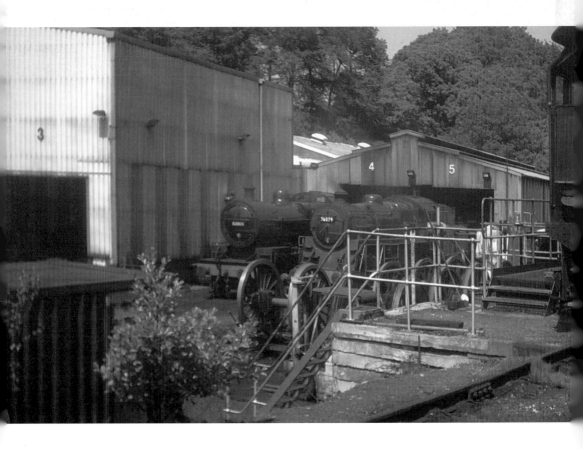

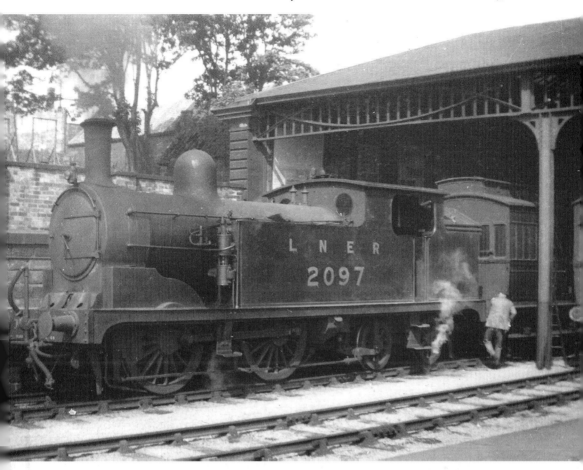

The end of the Esk Valley line, with LNER Class G5 No. 2079 preparing to depart from Whitby Town station with a local train in June 1934. (R. Carpenter collection)

Opposite top: No. 76079 prepares to take over from ex-GWR Churchward 2-8-0T No. 5224, which has brought its train in to Grosmont from Whitby for the onward journey to Pickering. (J. Thurston)

Opposite bottom: The NYMR collection of steam locomotives are housed in the shed and workshop at Grosmont, which is seen here in 2012, with No. 76079 and ex-Somerset & Dorset Joint Railway 7F 2-8-0 No. 53809 in view. (Author)

ACKNOWLEDGEMENTS

I should like to offer my grateful thanks to all who have assisted in putting this project together; it would have been more difficult without their help. Special thanks go to Mr R. Casserley, Roger Carpenter, Paul Hughes, LOSA, and John Thurston. Support was also given by Bernard Unsworth, who provided shed allocations, and Scarborough library.

My thanks also go to Hilary for her constant support and provision of tea and biscuits while I was busy working. Thanks also go to Gary and Keith for their support.

Finally, may I thank all of those whom I have forgotten to mention.